TROUT
STREAMS
OF
Western New York

J. MICHAEL KELLY

BURFORD BOOKS

Photos by J. Michael and Mary E. Kelly.

Printed in the United States of America.

10 9 8 7 6 5 4 3 2 1

Library of Congress Cataloging-in-Publication Data
is on file with the Library of Congress

TROUT
STREAMS
OF
Western New York

DEDICATION

Al Himmel of West Seneca was a chemist and teacher who spent a considerable share of his adult life indulging a deep passion for trout and trout waters. He especially loved to fly-fish the cold, clear streams which flowed within driving distance of home. Eventually, he wrote, printed and sold books about how and where to fish for trout close to Buffalo and Rochester. Since 2014, when Himmel passed away at the age of 89, collectors have been snatching up his copy-machine classics at yard sales, fishing-club meetings and other places where trout-lovers might feel at home. I found each of Al's books to be informative and entertaining. I think he would have enjoyed this one, too.

ACKNOWLEDGMENTS

The first time I fished the upper Genesee River near the Pennsylvania–New York border, I was heeding the suggestions of fellow anglers who, ironically, had begun to explore the trout waters of Department of Environmental Conservation Region 9 based on articles I had penned for *New York Game & Fish* magazine. These stories fell within the so-called "round-up" genre. They frequently included brief but useful descriptions of the Genesee, Wiscoy Creek and other western New York streams. My round-ups usually zeroed in on five to 10 trout-fishing destinations, all within a defined geographical area. The articles might be headed "Five Hot Summer Trout Streams in Western New York," or "Ten Top Late-Season Trout Rivers."

The trick, for this author and others who wanted to get consistent assignments with the magazine, was to steer clear of mindless repetition. You might see a stream featured in two or three round-ups over a span of several years, but it didn't sit well with the editor unless it offered some fresh destinations, too. These articles were staples of *Game & Fish*'s monthly issues. They were crammed with facts and "wish you were here" anecdotes about fast trout fishing. Most of my round-ups were about 2,000 to 2,500 words long, the equivalent of approximately nine or 10 type-written (or keyboarded) pages. Writers who sold regularly to *Game & Fish* were encouraged to fire up readers by supplying photos of big fish and phone numbers of tackle shops and regional DEC biologists who were on intimate terms with highlighted waters. Naturally, clear maps and precise road directions were vital.

The whole idea of the round-ups was to give readers so much information and encouragement that they would be strongly inclined to climb into their fishing cars and head for one or more of the profiled streams within days or even hours after reading the magazine.

My round-up advice was based mainly on personal experience, but the farther I traveled from my Syracuse-area home, the more I relied on the rollicking reminiscences which state fisheries biologists and local anglers shared with me. Their descriptions of tucked-away streams that I had previously managed to overlook added a sense of discovery to articles that otherwise could have been deadly dull. Over the years, I frequently consulted with DEC Region 9 fishing experts when I was researching stories about western New York streams. Some of the most reliable information came from Joe Evans, Mike Ermer and Scott Cornett. This trio kept me well informed about a variety of streams, mayfly hatches and other trout-related topics for more than 20 years.

Evans was sort of the old pro in the Region 9 office, like the go-to guy who makes the long walk to the pitcher's mound when his team needs one or two more outs to seal the deal. It was not unusual for a less experienced biologist or fish and wildlife tech to transfer my call to Joe when the questions veered off into uncharted territory. He seemed to be tuned-in to just about anything related to brooks, browns and rainbows, and I can't think of a major stream in western New York that Evans didn't know from beginning to end.

Ermer, although a long-time DEC employee, was not assigned to the Region 9 fisheries staff when I bumped into him. He was primarily a deer biologist, and happened to be a graduate of Syracuse University's Class of 1971—my class. When he picked up the phone one day when he was on desk duty at the Allegany field office, I remembered that I had spent my freshman year at Syracuse University's Watson West dormitory living on the same floor as a guy named Ermer. Would you believe that this Mike Ermer and the one I hadn't bumped into for at least 30 years were one and the same? Since I was a journalism major and Mike earned a degree from the State University of New York College of Environmental Science and Forestry, we were up and running in opposite directions well before our frosh year was finished. But as fate had it, we both enjoyed doing the same thing on our days away from school.

Yep, trout fishing. I know this only because I phoned the DEC that day for the specific purpose of talking about the Green Drake mayfly's place in western New York waters. After fielding my inquiry, Mike informed me that, while the fisheries guys were gone for the day, he regularly fished the Drakes himself. His personal knowledge and experiences sprinkled some extra zest on my written accounts of the big hatch.

As for Scott Cornett, when I first contacted him way back in the 1990s, he seemed to be on a mission to build a stockpile of trout-related research and reports that no outdoors writer could be without. Since then, his stacks and stacks of detailed reports on stream surveys—most of which are now available on-line—have helped him to become the foremost source of data on all things trout-ish in western New York. If you think I'm exaggerating his depth of knowledge regarding cold-water streams and their residents, call Scott at the DEC's Allegany office and test his knowledge about a trout topic of your choice. He'll either know the answer already or call back with the correct information within a few hours at most. At least, that's how it always works with me.

Scott, Mike and Joe—thank you. I couldn't have done this book without your help.

CONTENTS

INTRODUCTION

"There's no place like home."

So declared Dorothy, as she bid goodbye to the Land of Oz, clicked her red shoes together—and awoke from a remarkable dream, safe in her own bed, back in good old Kansas.

The Wizard of Oz, starring Judy Garland, is a classic motion picture, rightly admired by generations of fans. Yet the more times I see it on cable, the more it reminds me of trout streams and trout fishermen.

No, I have not lost my mind; at least, not that I know of. I fully understand that wandering around a strange country while singing cheerfully and hoping to meet an all-powerful wizard who can help our heroine find her way home is "just pretend." But that tiring trek is only slightly less sensible than driving half way across the United States in search of trout that are mostly smaller and fewer than the browns, brookies and rainbows that lurk in local waters.

Anglers who take quixotic journeys to distant streams while ignoring the fish-filled jewels that meander through nearby woods and meadows are usually convinced that their catch rates will improve if they would drive a little longer and cover a few more miles the next time they set forth with gear and tackle. Like Dorothy, they sometimes learn the hard way that home isn't so bad, at that.

Riffling through the pages of my thirty-some annual trout-fishing diaries, I am surprised to see how very few of my vacation trips to Michigan, Montana, Pennsylvania, the Canadian province of New

Brunswick and other bucket-list destinations ended in triumph. More often than not, my best fishing days in a given year were recorded soon after I had returned to New York from somewhere else!

Whether you are a New York resident or live so close to the Empire State that you can enjoy its trout fishing occasionally or even on a regular basis, there's a fair chance you might bump into me some time. This is a state which takes in the Adirondacks, the Catskills, the Hudson River valley and the Finger Lakes, to name a few fish-rich environs. There are thousands of streams within the bounds of New York that support wild trout, stocked trout or combinations of natural-born and hatchery-reared trout. I'd like to battle as many of these spotted and speckled beauties as I can while I live in this piscatorial paradise. If you understand what I'm saying here, and I am confident you do, there's just a slim chance we might meet on a mutually admired stream bank. We could share a bunch of war stories, you and me. But don't sit by your phone waiting for my "let's go fishing" call. Time is of the essence, because we New Yorkers will never have enough of that to cover all the close-to-home waters we desire to fish. We would need not one, but several lifetimes to accomplish such a task.

This book will help readers find their way around a largely over-looked area which merits serious exploration by local anglers as well as traveling sportsmen. *Trout Streams of Western New York* is about waters in DEC Region 9 that are unknown, underrated or strangely forgotten by most ordinary anglers and, believe it or not, even outdoors writers. It is like a guided tour of cold-water streams in Region 9, a tour which any angler who yearns to test quality trout waters in a systematic manner, one by one, will surely emulate. You will see that the book focuses on five of the six counties in the region which have inland trout streams within their borders. For our purposes, inland trout streams are those that are hospitable to wild or stocked trout throughout the year and do not move in or out of Lake Erie or Lake Ontario in order to spawn in the tributaries of those two Great Lakes.

Allegany, Cattaraugus, Chautauqua, Erie and Wyoming counties all have waters that fall within the inland trout stream definition. Niagara, the remaining county in Region 9, offers some terrific trout fishing for tourists, but has no true trout streams to call its own. To clarify, suppose

I needed a fish-in-hand photo of a brown trout to illustrate a book I was writing. Some skeptics will wonder why a 15-inch brown trout captured in East Koy Creek in Wyoming County might merit a long look, while a 15-*pound* brown trout caught in Niagara County's Eighteen Mile Creek would be precisely what we were *not* looking for. The whopper, as you might guess, resided in Lake Ontario most of the year, but swam into Eighteen Mile Creek during the annual autumn spawning run. The creek does not have the cold water temperatures, the bountiful food supply nor the well oxygenated currents that are necessary to maintain a year-round population of brown trout.

While you think that one over, ponder some statistics supplied by the DEC Region 9 trout maven, Scott Cornett, with a bit of help from the agency's Public Participation Specialist, Megan Gollwitzer:

- The region has 262 miles of stocked streams, including 155 miles that are stocked with two-year-old browns which average better than a foot long when they're released from hatcheries.

- In all, 52 streams in Region 9 are stocked, and 20 of those streams get an allocation of two-year-old hatchery browns, in addition to the standard batch of 8- or 9-inch yearlings.

- Region 9 stocking quotas in recent years have added up, on average, to more than 130,000 yearling browns plus 10,000 two-year-olds annually.

- Five hundred and forty-six streams in Region 9 hold populations of wild trout. (Some of the same waters receive hatchery-reared trout, too.)

- The region has 948 miles of streams that are inhabited by wild trout.

- Three hundred and thirty-five streams in the region hold at least a few wild browns. Some 334 streams are populated by wild brook trout, and quite a few of those have "very good numbers" of natives, according to Cornett. Also, 48 Region 9 streams are called "home" by natural-bred rainbows.

- Region 9's wild trout streams have very versatile habitat. Its regional total of 948 miles of streams of wild trout water includes 740 miles of water with wild browns, 542 miles of wild brook trout and 168 miles of wild rainbow streams. Obviously, some of this mileage overlaps; for example, a specific creek might be home to both brown and brook trout, brown and rainbow trout, brookies and rainbows, or even all three species.

- Finding places to fish for trout in Region 9 is not overly difficult. More than 170 miles of streambanks in the region are marked with yellow signs that denote the presence of public fishing rights (PFR), and many other stream sections are open to fishermen who ask the landowners for permission. Even where the land along a stream is marked with "no fishing," "no trespassing" or similar warning signs, permission to trespass is sometimes granted to those who politely ask for it.

Access opportunities in the region also include dozens of streams within the 65,000-acre Allegany State Park, in Cattaraugus County. The park, located immediately south of Salamanca and the Seneca Indian reservation, is not a blue-ribbon fishery, but its tumbling little streams have the makings of a very pleasant trip for any angler who likes to creep along the water's edge and blend into the background so that wary fish can't readily detect him. Trout that shy are among the stealthiest prey species a skilled trout fisher will ever encounter.

None of the regional fisheries units that the DEC uses to track changes in fish populations and analyze aquatic habitats throughout New York does a more thorough job than the Region 9 crew. Some of its best work is displayed on the DEC website, which can be accessed at http://www.dec.ny.gov. Using your cursor, click on "Recreation," "Freshwater fishing," "places to fish," "Western NY Fishing," "Wild Trout Streams," "Stocked Streams in Western New York," and other stops to find any information you might need to wrap up the planning for your next trout trip. The DEC Region 9 staff has provided further help to fishermen by filing detailed reports on their annual electrofishing surveys with the Albany higher-ups. Dozens of western New York trout streams have acquired important friends by being featured in the region's field reports.

By merely looking at the photos of 20-inch browns examined during some of those fall forays, you will understand why I enjoyed writing those round-up articles so much. You will share Dorothy's appreciation of home, sweet home, I bet.

Enjoy the book. I wish you the best of luck during your future trout-fishing expeditions, whether the grail you seek is hours away or plainly visible from your back porch. The cold streams of western New York will be a great place to begin or conclude your quest, but as fishermen have urged one another for many decades, please leave a few trout for me.

PART I

GO WEST, YOU ANGLERS!

Some historians doubt the event ever occurred, but legend has it that Horace Greeley, the most influential American newspaperman of the mid-19th century, once was confronted by a young reader who was unsure where his future lay. When this lad stopped whining and wringing his hands, Greeley supposedly gave him some advice, of the short, sweet and pointed variety.

"Go west, young man, go west," the journalist has been quoted.

Aside from an occasional editorial, the visionary leader of the most-circulated American newspaper of the 1860s and early '70s did not have to crack bullwhips to send settlers scurrying across the Great Plains and Indian territories in search of their destinies. Most of the pioneers, outlaws, prospectors and other adventuresome people who clambered aboard wagon trains and followed rutted trails through the wilderness did not need much encouragement. They were chasing their dreams, and in many cases found exactly what they were hoping for.

Greeley died in 1872, just seven years after the Civil War ended at the Appomattox Court House. He was a cheerleader for those who rode Conestoga wagons through seas of tall grass to go as far west as they dared.

At the time of Greeley's passing, many thousands of persons had already been lured westward by visions of land, free for the taking, which was said to be so full of gold nuggets that streams and rocky hillsides glittered like melting icicles in the hot summer sun. I would like to be able to say that anglers from the Catskills and Adirondacks in southeastern and northern New York joined the settlers' caravans with visions of lakes and rivers full of trout.

Unfortunately, very few pioneers headed west with plans to fish for fun or sustenance, either. Not even the fur trappers who explored the Great Plains and the Rockies were conservationists in the classic sense, although the legendary "mountain men" who often had trout on their cooking fires knew the wisdom of eating every bite of food that nature provided them. And they did so, often learning from the Indian tribes they encountered. Even some of the bones saved from a thoroughly cooked rainbow or cutthroat trout might be used in place of a sewing needle, or even as a fish hook, if the real thing were not available. As the years passed, many fishermen headed into the unknown with small boxes of tackle tucked into their wagons or saddlebags, and, using the journals of Lewis and Clark as guides and mentors, made sure to try their luck in rivers that were said to be teeming with cutthroat trout.

Back east, many streams in western New York held plenty of native brook trout through the 19th century and the 20th, as well. Who, knowing that every brookie or "speckled trout" reeled in, netted or speared to feed a farmer's family would interfere with such an operation? And weren't the fish essentially unlimited, population-wise? Pollution was probably more damaging to the resource than over-fishing, and the frequent enterprise of clearing large blocks of forests to use in construction of homes or the erection of tanneries met with few, if any, objections from pioneers or other western expansionists.

Happily for all—trout included—the Conservation Movement, led by President Teddy Roosevelt, Gifford Pinchot and many other far-sighted individuals, advocated wise use of natural resources just in the nick of time. By the early 1900s, re-forestation was well underway in many parts of the northeastern United States, and the stream currents that used to ripple with wild trout were born again as fish hatcheries stocked thousands upon thousands of natives for the angler's pleasure. In fact, many state and private trout farms were able to produce generous quotas of brown trout from eggs obtained from Germany and England. Fish culturists cranked out rainbows imported from the Rocky

Mountain states, as well. One of the premier fish-rearing facilities in its time—and our time, too—was sold to the New York Fish Commission in 1868 by its designer, Seth Green. Built on the bank of Spring Creek in Caledonia, the hatchery was refurbished a few years ago. Its personnel now crank out two-year-old brown trout for release in streams across the state. The 13- to 15-inch browns from the Spring Creek holding tanks are among the prettiest and hard-fighting hatchery-reared trout in the country, and much appreciated by the anglers who catch them.

Very few of the fishermen who journeyed west in the 1800s had more than a hazy picture of the rivers and trout that would help feed their families and provide countless hours of recreation for homesteaders and adventurers. Looking back, Greeley's advice to that restless *Tribune* reader seems sound to me, whether the old newsman's musings were straightforward or apocryphal. It was wise counsel for anglers, as well as pioneers with itchy feet. Fishermen, including yours truly, can't help but wonder what stream curls around the next hill and what sort of trout it holds. Anglers living in New York tend to expand their horizons westward, first of all because they started in the East, and second, because their fathers, grandfathers and other descendants blazed the way for them.

Today, trout fishermen seldom fish to feed their families, but their urgent personal need to explore new waters prompts many to stow a rod and reel, ready for use, in the cars they drive home after a hard day at work. Some of these fellows (and not a few women anglers) find time to make a few casts during a daily lunch break. Others will hit a favorite stream during the rush hour, and the real enthusiasts may telephone a spouse now and then to request permission for a prolonged outing, followed, of course, by dinner at a favorite family restaurant.

Finally, I have noticed that many city-living businessmen and women no longer assume that a local golf course is the perfect place to cement a big deal with a new client or customer. By asking a few questions ("Does Mr. Smith do any fishing?") a canny sales person can ink a long-term contract and make a life-long friend, too.

Invite your prospective customer to try a nearby stream or two that you know better than most, but don't reveal too many secrets until you become well acquainted. Maybe your networking on the job will yield information about a stream that is a far piece from home, but not so far west that you can't get there from here. Residents of Maine are notorious for giving directions of a vague or confusing nature, but fishermen everywhere seem to be born with a talent for obfuscating about the location of a productive river, let alone a pet pool. You will probably have to ask the same questions several times to get the answers you are looking for, so be prepared to give your new customer-fishing buddy a lengthy grilling. Go west, like Mr. Greeley said, only don't use your cell phone or any other electronic devices on your way there. Refrain from rubbernecking when you travel with trout gear, lest others using the United States of America's unsurpassed network of highways take notice of your suspicious behavior. Our waters are crowded enough already, thank you. We have miles to go before we sleep.

As another 19th century wandering sage (and fine bait fisherman) might have put it, "Mum's the word, Huck."

Please take appropriate action to safeguard your favorite western New York streams. Many of these waters have been under-fished for many years. However, they could well be on the verge of re-discovery. DEC Region 9's superb smaller streams are easy to miss, in part because the bigger roads connecting the Southern Tier and Niagara Frontier counties tend to funnel fishermen through the semi-rural regions instead of compelling them to stay awhile. The bigger trout streams in the western part of the state, including the upper Genesee River, Wiscoy Creek and Clear Creek near Arcade, are beloved by anglers who live nearby and think of them as their home waters. Yet these exciting fisheries are largely unknown to fishermen who live in Central New York (the Syracuse area), the Adirondack Park and the Catskill mountains.

There is no shame in such a lack of appreciation, but it is surprising in an era when fishermen have remarkable access to information about distant streams and all sorts of angling techniques, via books, regional and national magazines, and most of all, computer chat rooms and websites. The Internet, for those who have yet to appreciate its charms, gives anglers what amounts to an instant connection with fishing experts the world over. Using the 'Net, sportsmen with a knack for such things can now troll for tips about where, when and how to fish for any species, at a time and place of their convenience. It amazes me, though, to realize that many anglers seem to use web sites and chat rooms to peddle false information to others.

I used to be a regular visitor to an on-line forum which encouraged participants—most of whom lived in states other than New York—to share information about recent catches of note, fly patterns that were fooling lots of trout during the evening hatch, and so forth. I was a fairly frequent observer but an indifferent contributor, at best, because many emails aired on this forum quickly confirmed my worries that some of the participants were pumping out false information as fast as they could. Their intent, I believe, was to give chat-room sportsmen the idea that mayfly hatches in the region were sparse, the trout weren't hitting anyway, and everybody reading these words should postpone scheduled trips until the action picked up. In truth, the fishing was reasonably good, the hatches were variable and skilled fly fishers were doing better than fair. The plotters were lying to a bunch of gullible strangers, in order to keep area fishing hotspots to themselves.

I would never try to deceive a fellow angler that way, would you?

CHAPTER ONE

Chautauqua County

Promoters of fishing tourism in Chautauqua County sing the praises of muskellunge, walleyes, smallmouth bass and panfish—usually in that order. I don't blame them at all for not mentioning trout-fishing opportunities very often. I understand completely that it's easy to sell short-term visitors on booking cabins, campgrounds and motel rooms that are within walking distance of Lake Erie or Chautauqua Lake. In contrast, anyone would admit it is quite a trick to sell trout fishermen on the chance to catch a few wild browns in a creek that goes dry some summers.

It's what most publicists would call a no-brainer. Lake Erie and Chautauqua Lake hold numerous bronzebacks, some weighing more than seven pounds; and bass share the neighborhood in both lakes with 10-pound walleyes and muskies that sometimes are long enough to break the 50-inch barrier. Who wouldn't travel long distances to joust with fish like that?

In comparison, the gorgeous browns that inhabit *Clear Creek*—the one that originates in the vicinity of the Boutwell Hill State Forest and flows southeast through Ellington—might grow to a maximum length of 22 inches or so, if they can dodge fishermen's hooks and elude mink, herons and other predators from one summer to the next. In July and August, many of the browns living downstream from Ellington must swim like the Dickens to get out of that stretch before it dries up. The water goes underground, no doubt confusing many anglers and trout, alike, and it typically stays out of sight for a mile or so below the exit hole. By the end of the summer, the creek pops out again, and the researchers who keep track of the phenomenon typically find that the missing groundwater is in the very trout-friendly, low-50 degree range when it re-emerges. Here's more on this intriguing stream, and some other beauties in Chautauqua County.

CLEAR CREEK (ELLINGTON)

RATING: ★★★★ (4 stars, with 1 star being the minimum and 5 the difficult-to-obtain maximum score.) The ratings in this book reflect the views of the author, alone.

BEST METHOD: Spinning, with ultralight tackle and long casts required.

BEST TIME TO FISH: After the disappearing sections of the creek have reappeared.

As a trout devotee, I find Clear Creek's now-you-see-it, now-you-don't character fascinating. The only thing about the creek that impressed me more during my initial visit to the Ellington area was a DEC fisheries unit leader's quick rundown on places where I could get in and out of that cold late-summer water without disturbing fish or landowners. It turns out that almost the entire length of the stream—approximately 10.4 miles—is open to public fishing. Even better, several angler parking lots are conveniently located along Route 62, between 2 and 3 miles upstream from the village.

The DEC Region 9's reigning trout wizard, biologist Scott Cornett, knows Clear Creek (and many other western New York streams) inside and out. It is, therefore, quite convincing when he raves about the Ellington stream. He calls it "by far the best place" in Chautauqua County for those who are mainly interested in wild trout, rather than stocked fish. He has collected and scale-sampled many plump browns in the 12- to 14-inch range, and, during recent mid-summer electro-fishing campaigns, a few out-and-out monsters that measured better than 20 inches.

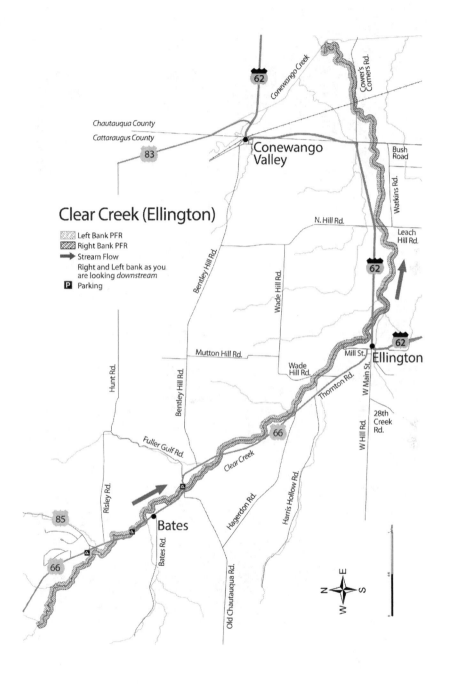

Clear Creek (Ellington)

▨ Left Bank PFR
▨ Right Bank PFR
➡ Stream Flow
Right and Left bank as you
are looking *downstream*
🅿 Parking

Conewango Creek

62

Chautauqua County
Cattaraugus County

83

Conewango
Valley

Cower's Corners Rd.

Bush
Road

Watkins Rd.

N. Hill Rd.

Leach
Hill Rd.

Bentley Hill Rd.

Wade Hill Rd.

62

62

Mutton Hill Rd.

Mill St.

Ellington

Wade
Hill Rd.

Thornton Rd.

W Main St.

Hunt Rd.

Bentley Hill Rd.

28th
Creek
Rd.

W Hill Rd.

Fuller Gulf Rd.

Clear Creek

66

Harris Hollow Rd.

Hagerdon Rd.

Risley Rd.

85

Bates

Bates Rd.

66

Old Chautauqua Rd.

N E
W S

A volunteer member of the DEC's field crew admires a 22-inch brown trout collected during electrofishing studies on Clear Creek, a prime fishing hole near Ellington in Chautauqua County.

One of those hot-weather trips generated data that showed Clear Creek to be populated by approximately 935 adult fish—in general, browns five inches or longer—per mile. Most of the creek looks good and fishes even better, with numerous bends, plunge pools, log jams and undercuts that nice-sized browns are lucky to call home, sweet home. Averaging about 20–25 feet across, the creek is heavily vegetated in the Cowen Corners section. Although the creek is not especially large, and feels the heat of a long summer, it can be explored very efficiently in July or August, by someone who knows to handle light or ultralight tackle. Clear Creek has enough openings and angles in its moderately dense bank cover to permit bait, lure and fly fishing specialists to do their respective things. Any small streamer fly with a few prominent splashes of white fur or feathers tied into it will catch trout here—but you definitely will have to work for them, more days than not. Start off with a size 8 white Muddler or perhaps a blacknose dace imitation.

Cornett says Clear Creek is fishable year-round, except for the part which pulls the disappearing act in the summer. Along both banks from the mouth up to the headwaters near the Cockaigne Ski Center, Clear Creek has bank cover which ranges from sparse to dense, with a mix of overgrown fields and first or second-growth hardwood forests. There's plenty of shade to hide furtive brown trout, but not so much that anglers can't find a safe, comfortable path downstream or up when the fish are active and you want to keep moving along while conditions are right.

The nagging problems on Clear Creek are its fairly steep gradient and loose banks. When the creek comes up suddenly or stays high for more than a day or two it is prone to damaging wash-outs. Ironically, one of the best times to try this underrated stream is when heavy showers cause it to rise and turn color. These factors, in turn, are likely to trigger a feeding spree, as trout move out of their regular hiding places and nose into the heads of large pools and patches of smooth water. In these places, many of which are no more than a foot deep, big browns will gorge on natural foods—worms, minnows, mayflies and so on—and they don't stop until they are just too full to take even one more tidbit from the current. As the water rises and then recedes, familiar pools and runs get unneeded makeovers, and anglers feel compelled to re-learn the water's course before fishing it again.

A necklace dam, made of carefully placed boulders, improved trout holding capacity and habitat in Clear Creek near Arcade.

Cornett calls this cycle of erosion and migrating stream beds "here today and there tomorrow," which strikes me as a vivid but accurate description of the gully-washing tendency shared by many New York trout waters.

To find this stream, take Route 60 south from Fredonia for about 18 miles, to the hamlet of Gerry. At Gerry, turn left onto Route 50, and follow that road approximately 12 miles, to Ellington. Clear Creek is visible from Route 50 just east of Ellington; and also from Route 66 as you drive upstream from Ellington to Thornton, the site of the Cockaigne Ski Center. You can follow Clear Creek all the way into Ellington, and from there, on into Cattaraugus County and the junction with Conewango Creek. The latter, in the town of Conewango, is a good spot for muskies and bass but not for trout.

Newcomers to Clear Creek should be aware of special regulations that permit anglers to fish for trout outside of the state season. Specifically, it's okay to wet a line for the stream's abundant browns following a no-kill, flies-or-lures only rule from October 16–March 31. Don't expect much company, as angling pressure in most Western New York streams is extremely light at this time of the year.

CHERRY CREEK

RATING: ★★★ (3 stars)
BEST METHOD: Use live bait with the hook's barb flattened to make quick release easier.
BEST TIME TO FISH: Immediately after a drenching rain colors the water.

Fishermen who enjoy poking around small streams that draw their nearly transparent flows from underground springs will feel right at home on the banks of Cherry Creek. Like Clear Creek, it's a tributary of Conewango Creek. During a recent summertime survey, DEC crews estimated this 10-foot-wide stream harbored approximately 500 adult brown trout per mile. The creek is not currently stocked, which means anything you catch there was stream-born. Most of the wild browns in Cherry Creek are between six and 12 inches. According to DEC researchers, the best fishing in this stream is from its mouth to about half a mile above the village of Cherry Creek.

If you would like to explore this lightly fished water, be sure to ask permission from property owners, for Cherry Creek has no public fishing signs posted along its banks. Few "no fishing" signs are tacked on trees or fence posts along the creek, either, and that is usually a signal that the person who says yes or no simply likes to know who is on the stream, and what sort of folks they might be. The stream isn't easy to fish; in fact, its trout have a reputation for wariness, probably due to the sun-splashed pools and gentle currents that prevail for most of its length. Brown trout love shade and knee-deep pools, but they have a low tolerance for anglers who spray water and clash rocks together. Give such fish the respect they have earned, and don't take too many wizened browns for the pan. Let most of your catch go back to the water after you've fooled them with your bait and tactical skills.

This locally-known stream flows through a crossroads community which is also dubbed "Cherry Creek." To add to the confusion, the surrounding local township is also "Cherry Creek." And the namesake stream runs through both town and hamlet, naturally. But getting around this neck of the New York woods is easy, if you merely re-read the directions I supplied for Clear Creek, just a couple of pages back. On page 40 of your DeLorme New York Atlas &

Gazetteer, look almost due north for about 5.5 miles from Clear Creek village and you can see where Cherry Creek runs along Farrington Hollow Road.

GOOSE CREEK

RATING: ★★★ (3 stars)

BEST METHOD: Salted minnows should produce, although there's an opportunity to take trout on streamers and bucktails that resemble the natural food.

BEST TIME TO FISH: Get up early, because the fish population peaks early in the season, and that's when you can prowl along the banks in search of fat, stocked two-year-olds.

In contrast to Cherry Creek (and Clear Creek, too), Goose Creek is easily one of the most heavily fished trout waters in Chautauqua County. The angling pressure is a direct result of regular spring-time stockings that take place in the creek, as well as the close proximity of the stream and the county's more populous towns, namely Ashville and Jamestown. Regardless of reasons, visitors looking for some trout fishing should be aware that Goose Creek takes a pounding in April, but pressure usually drops off dramatically after mid-May. I suspect the opening of seasons for other species, especially black crappies and walleyes, gets the attention of local fishermen from that point forward.

To me, Goose Creek is a vivid example of what put-and-take fishing is, and what it isn't and probably never will be. The DEC hatcheries at Randolph and Caledonia raise annual crops of trout for release in dozens of fishy-looking rivers and creeks scattered throughout western New York. In the spring, about 3,000 trout—including 1,550 yearling browns averaging around 8 inches long, another 400 two-year-old brownies, and 1,050 yearling brook trout—are shown the door at the hatcheries. These fish, and in particular the two-year-olds that measure between 12 and 15 inches when they are stocked, thrive for a month or two in Goose Creek, which has good cover and plenty of food to sustain trout. Some wild browns, although not many, share pools in the stream with stocked browns, and a few of those fish may outlive typical stockers. All this is good news for trout fishermen. But hot weather and lukewarm currents do not bode well for anglers in the long run.

By early June, temperatures in Goose Creek warm to the point that they become marginal by trout standards, with thermometer readings climbing into the 70s around high noon. Some years temperatures are a little cooler, but not by much. Trout in residence seek out the mouths of tributary streams, spring seeps, swift runs that have high oxygen levels compared to readings in slower currents and even areas that are exceptionally shady. But only a fraction of stocked trout will hold over in Goose Creek and other barely suitable habitat. Just which fish survive from one year to the next depends, ultimately, on how tepid the water gets, and whether it cools down in a couple of days or several weeks. While newcomers should not expect first-class fishing in the summer months, it is not at all unusual for patient anglers to catch a few trout following a cloudburst, even after the 4th of July. In fact, Goose Creek is approximately 10 miles long. It empties into Chautauqua Lake in the village of Ashville, which can be pinpointed by following Route 394 west from Jamestown. Some of the creek's most tantalizing sections are found between the village of Panama and Blockville, where the stream flows in an easterly direction along Randolph Road and Route 474. Most of the 5 miles of public fishing access on the stream is in this stretch.

The creek is about 20 feet wide, on average, and it has an interesting mix of pools and riffles where stocked or wild browns can find lots of aquatic insects, small dace and other food. At times, its forested banks can be a source of frustration for back-casting fly-rodders, but minnow imitations should provoke a nice brown just about any day during the trout season. Ultralight lures such as a silver and black Panther Martin or a gold Phoebe spoon will usually get some looks and follows, and if a solid strike doesn't ensue within a few more casts, try a garden worm on a number 6 hook. That's a "bait and switch" good for fooling trout everywhere, including Goose Creek.

PRENDERGAST CREEK

RATING: ★★★ (3 stars)

BEST TIME: A cloudy, cool, rainy day late in June.

BEST METHOD: With wild browns in the 20-inch range lurking in deeper pools around the mouth of Wing Creek, a tributary, use minnows or minnow imitations at sunrise or sunset, especially in mid-summer.

Where else but in New York could a fine trout stream flow within walking distance of a nationally renowned muskellunge hatchery? On many mornings in April or May, Department of Environmental Conservation workers are checking nets along the west shore of Chautauqua Lake for new arrivals. Meanwhile, the fish technicians strip eggs from hen muskies. The hard work that goes with the job for hatchery employees pays off when the eggs hatch and, months later, 8- to 11-inch-long muskies of the Chautauqua Lake strain are ready for stocking in rivers and lakes, most but not all of them located in the westernmost counties in New York. The hatchery is at Prendergast Point, and the trout stream I'm telling you about is Prendergast Creek. It is one of a very few significant cold-water tributaries that flow into the west side of Chautauqua Lake.

So as not to mislead readers, I'd like to mention a couple of Prendergast Creek's shortcomings, as well as some obvious attributes. First of all, the stream has only about 2 miles of fishable water, and none of that is marked for public fishing rights. You definitely should knock on a few doors to get permission to fish before you rig up your trout tackle.

Prendergast Creek is not a great trout stream, but downstream from its confluence with a cold-water tributary called Wing Creek, the fishing improves significantly. Upstream from the junction, Prendergast Creek is too warm to support many trout in the summer. However, Wing Creek is cold enough to keep the resident trout active, hungry and growing. When the Region 9 trout management crew last assayed Prendergast in 2013, they found about 175 wild, adult trout per mile, including one 21-inch beauty. One of the most interesting discoveries during that outing was evidence that some of the larger browns in the creek have taken to leaving the creek now and then to feed in the open water of Chautauqua Lake.

This creek, like many others in Western New York, it is managed with the help of special regulations that reflect light angling pressure and other local realities. The rules for Prendergast Creek permit anglers to enjoy it on a catch-and-release basis between regular trout seasons. Only flies or spinning lures may be used from October 16 through March 31 on this creek.

You can get to Prendergast Creek by following Route 394 along the west shore of Chautauqua Lake to the state muskellunge hatchery at Prendergast Point. It's roughly a 10-mile drive from Jamestown to the DEC fish factory. Across the road from the hatchery entrance, hang a left onto Davis Road and start scouting for fishy-looking sections of the creek.

MILL CREEK

RATING: ★★★ (3 stars)

BEST TIME TO FISH: Early morning in mid-summer. Get there before the sun warms the local brown trout hiding places.

BEST METHODS: To catch the brook trout that are stocked in a stretch of Mill Creek below Sinclairville, try your smallest in-line spinners. Silver blades are your best bet.

I am confident every state in the Union, with the possible exceptions of Hawaii and Alaska, has at least one popular fishing hole named "Mill Creek." New York has several that I know of, including two, between Patchinville and Perkinsville in Steuben County, and a third located near Boonville in Oneida County, that are among the better trout fishing spots in their region. That's also the case with **Mill Creek** in Chautauqua County. Stocked annually with about 800 yearling brook trout and around 100 two-year-old browns from the DEC hatchery system, this stream would be a very productive fishing hole if it didn't get so warm during the summer. Unfortunately, summer water thermometer readings in the mid-70s are not unusual in Mill Creek. Once or twice a year, heavy rain and run-off scours the creek bottom and forces area fishermen to relearn the contours of the stream.

Chautauqua County's Mill Creek is a Cassadaga Creek tributary which runs about 25 feet wide on average. The creek flows through the village of Sinclairville, and slides beneath state Route 60. About 2.4 miles of the stream, mostly in or around the village, are stocked. If you have a winning personality and are a good salesman, don't be afraid to ask a landowner for permission to try your luck on his or her property. Most fishermen seem to be shy about knocking on doors or even calling out and asking directions from their vehicles. What do they have to lose? Try asking whether you are going the right way to State Route 60 or should make a U-turn, instead. It might be the ice-breaker you need to start a genuine friendship with somebody who owns a promising piece of trout water. And, you can rest assured, the same strategy will pay off on other fishing holes as the years go by.

Like Clear Creek, some of Mill Creek takes an annual dive. It happens during a prolonged or intense dry spell, when part of the shriveled stream goes underground, in the vicinity of the Route 60 bridge. Some years, the vanishing is of brief duration, and the water is back "up" within a few days. In other seasons, the creek could be out of sight for weeks, in the usual places. Either way, when the flow re-appears, the water temperature is likely to register in the 50s.

Some dandy fish can be caught when the creek's missing currents come back. Readers should not be shocked if some 14- or 15-inch wild browns turn up in the bone-dry pools that re-fill with cold water. This normally happens around Labor Day, provided the local streams are getting some decent rain showers and air and water temperatures are cooling off.

If you are thinking about taking a summer trip to Mill Creek or other streams much like it, figure on getting to the water early in the day, ideally just as the sun is starting to peek over the wooded hillsides in western New York. The trout will, more often than not, be up and at 'em when you pull off onto the road shoulder or a designated parking area. They will be hunting something meaty, such as a large crayfish or a small horned dace. Unfortunately, the fun will be over fairly soon. By 9 a.m. at the latest, even the quick, nibbling attack of assorted chubs will be pretty well finished. It's nothing you said or did.

Rather, water temperatures increase quickly on a bright, sunny day, and as that happens, trout appetites will diminish.

Anglers who like to sleep late will have their innings at the start of the season. The most comfortable times of the day in early or mid-April are between 10 a.m. and 2 p.m.—usually. One never knows for sure about any weather forecast until everything that is supposed to happen actually occurs. But on-stream experience, and stacks of 30-plus personal fishing diaries, tells me that trout stream temperatures typically rise a few degrees before noon and creep up a little bit more by 3 or 4 o'clock in the afternoon.

OTHER CHAUTAUQUA COUNTY TROUT STREAMS

Having just presented you with short but useful reviews of streams where even a casual angler can hook a couple of nice browns during a weekend visit or on the way home from work, it might be helpful to keep a couple of "Plan B" side-trips handy, just in case. There are plenty of other trout waters in Chautauqua County that are worth visiting. For starters, **Farrington Hollow Brook** is an overlooked treasure, about 20 feet wide, with both stocked and wild brown trout. At the points where it glides under culverts at Wentworth Road and Hamlet Road, it is just west of the hamlet named "Hamlet." (And no, I'm not kidding. This corner of Chautauqua County has lots of odd but interesting names, including communities and crossroads that show up on area maps as "Skunks Corner," "Wango," and "Kabob.") Suffice to say, the squiggly blue lines around such places are always worth pulling over, taking a look and dropping a bait in the water—unless the spot is surrounded by "no trespassing" signs.

Many streams that look good for trout aren't. Yet DEC biologists and conservation officers, and yours truly will attest that western New York takes in quite a few creeks, brooks, and so forth which are overlooked if not completely forgotten by a majority of modern trout-lovers. To name one Dunkirk area stream that could use a few more fishermen, how about **Canadaway Creek**? It's just a hop, skip and a cast southeast of Fredonia. This book, like the others I've published previously under the Burford Books label, is about *inland* trout streams, that is, those which are *not* tributaries of New York's share of the Great Lakes. I left Lake Erie and Lake Ontario out of my trout books because they are big enough and sufficiently puzzling to merit separate coverage. Canadaway, which has a very productive Lake Erie steelhead run, is mentioned briefly here, but that's because the big rainbows from the lake can't make it up and over the falls at Laona.

The upper part of the creek, which can't be reached by lake-run rainbows unless they get a big helping hand, or maybe a big fish ladder, likely would serve for steelhead spawning, but at this writing is stocked with a tiny quota of 300 brookies and browns. The creek has a strong following among fly-rodders in the Fredonia area, and many of them truly enjoy the relative calm and solitude that exists in certain places where steelhead do *not* make themselves at home.

Other trout waters in Chautauqua County worth a try if you live in the county or are just passing through, include **Cassadaga Creek**, which has 5.4 miles of public fishing areas between the village of Cassadaga and a crossroad called Kabob, with access points off Luce, Moon, Putnam and Waterman roads; and the **West Branch of Conewango Creek**, a mostly posted stream off Route 83 in the town of Villanova which is fishable all year for those who get permission from adjoining landowners.

CHAPTER TWO

Cattaraugus County

These days, anglers are told they must put up with litter bugs, fish hogs and other "sportsmen" they encounter on the river because "a trout stream needs friends." Admittedly, the phrase rings true, because our cold-water resources are inherently fragile and can stand only so much pollution, predation, and fishing pressure before decline and ruination are irreversible. However, there is more than one kind of friend. Some deserve an angler's admiration and others do not. The kind we should give a wide berth, as a rule, are self-proclaimed friends, who express their burning desire to work diligently for the cause of the day, but are dependably absent when the day of reckoning is at hand.

A buddy of mine always carries a plastic bag with him when he goes fishing. He picks up after guys who won't. He also turns in a poacher, if he happens to see one, and telephones a conservation officer afterward to see what became of his complaint. When he reads something about a trout-fishing trend that worries him, whether he spotted it in a national outdoors magazine or in a local newspaper, he responds with a thoughtful letter to the editor. Most important, he treats his brother and sister anglers—and their secret places—with respect.

This is the sort of friend a trout stream really can use, especially if that stream flows through an urban or suburban environment where many anglers aren't aware of traditional concepts such as sharing the water, limiting your catch and passing on our time-honored angling traditions. This one teaches by example.

CATTARAUGUS CREEK

RATING: ★★★★ (4 stars)

BEST TIME TO FISH: After a heavy rain shower is over and the creek is slowly settling down. Gully-washers almost always trigger some action for steelhead downstream of the dam, and for browns and rainbows in the various creeks above that structure.

BEST METHOD: Cast a wet fly with pulsing hackles down and across the Catt's currents. Let it linger below you for a few seconds before starting a slow, hand-twist retrieve.

Like many other trout fishers, I am conflicted about a state and federal proposal to lower the old Springville hydro dam (known locally as "Scoby Dam") on Cattaraugus Creek roughly in half, about 20 feet. The remodeled structure would include a fish ladder to allow passage of incoming steelhead or block migration of spawning sea lampreys as deemed necessary. When it's operational, the revised dam would put Lake Erie-strain steelhead in reach of another 31 miles of spawning grounds. The popular species currently spawns in about 34 miles of gravel between the mouth of Cattaraugus Creek and the Springville dam in Erie County. And, although trout fishers are usually reluctant to squabble among each other in matters like these, it seems very likely that if there is to be a winner in the Springville fracas, big steelies will prevail over the wild and stocked brown, brook and rainbow trout that have previously held sway in the upper reaches of Cattaraugus Creek.

My question, for the more ardent advocates of dam modification or removal, is a simple one—namely, where trout fishing is involved, is bigger necessarily better?

The answer boils down to the values systems of individual anglers. I grant you, anybody who puts in a few days at or below Scoby Dam will have an opportunity, sooner or later, to hook up with a personal-best steelhead. Such a fish could easily be 30 inches long and weigh 10 pounds, and the steelheader who brings it to net according to the rules of fair chase; that is, no snagging or "lifting," has my respect and that of most other anglers, too. So I ask you readers, once again, is bigger better?

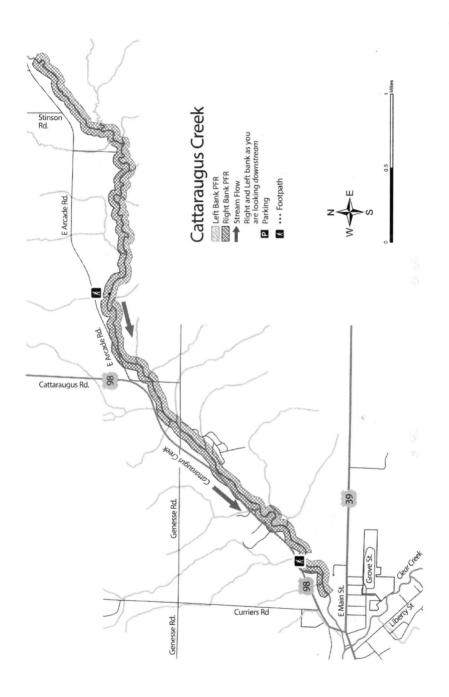

Cattaraugus Creek

Stinson Rd.

E Arcade Rd.

E Arcade Rd.

Cattaraugus Rd.

98

Cattaraugus Creek

Genesse Rd.

39

Grove St.

Clear Creek

98

E Main St.

Genesse Rd.

Curriers Rd

Liberty St

Left Bank PFR
Right Bank PFR
Stream Flow
Right and Left bank as you
are looking downstream
P   Parking
🔍 ··· Footpath

N
W   E
S

0   0.5   1
Miles

Those lobbying for new spawning areas above the dam predict steelhead anglers and the regional sport-fishing economy would be big winners if such an undertaking came to fruition. The losers, everyone seems to agree, would be small-stream trout and the breed of sportsmen who love foot-long fish more than king-size steelhead and salmon. Experts are mostly in agreement that steelies given admission to the water above the Scoby Dam would put their stamp of ownership on the new spawning grounds by chasing wild browns, rainbows and brookies from the most desirable egg-laying habitat and occupying the best available feeding lanes and hiding places throughout "the Catt" and its tributaries. The takeover could be accomplished faster than many fishermen realize.

Because this book is about *inland* trout streams, and not the tributaries of Lake Erie, I've elected to write in depth about lower Cattaraugus Creek some other time. However, since the fish-passage devices have wide implications for approximately 65 miles of the Catt, it seems only right that I would briefly summarize the project at this time. As it happened, a fellow writer got to the controversy ahead of me, and did a fine job of breaking down the whole mess.

In a nicely balanced article which appeared in *Fly Fisherman* magazine in 2016, fishing guide and freelance writer Karl Weixlmann got to the heart of the issue when he pointed out that 17 miles of the Catt and 27 miles of its tributaries above the dam sustain populations of wild brown and/or rainbow trout. In addition, at least 15 of the streams in the headwaters of the creek support native brook trout. Although Weixlmann was careful not to put it this way, the Cattaraugus Creek dam project may wind up as a roll of the dice, with an unpredictable outcome. Once lowered to facilitate big-fish passage, the dam is unlikely ever to be rebuilt according to its original specifications, and the downfall of the Scoby Dam would, for practical purposes, give Lake Erie's buck steelhead a standing invitation to try their luck with the ladies on the gravel beds upstream from Springville.

If the silver bullets can simply find their way around that dam—and the big-money people are counting on it—steelhead and steelhead fishermen will, thereafter, rule most of the pools and riffles of Cattaraugus Creek and the grand share of its feeder streams, to boot. The migratory steelies will be able to run rough-shod over the 10-inchers that are most prevalent in the water above the big dam, but the access situation is not entirely clear. Maybe all of us ought to calm down a little before we start talking. We do know, as of late December in 2016, that the Catt is owned by the Seneca Nation of Indians from Gowanda downstream nearly to its mouth. Non-Senecas must purchase fishing licenses from one of the tribal convenience stores before wetting a line in search of the Catt's steelhead. Several dirt roads in or near Gowanda lead from Route 438 to the river. Another section affords access to 15 miles of the creek, from the dam downstream. Its swift currents and wide, slate-bottom pools can be tricky to wade, most notably when recent rains have muddied the water.

Above the dam, Cattaraugus Creek and feeder streams sport New York's green and yellow "public fishing" signs that always let strangers know they are welcome—even though they have no guarantee of actually catching something. If you're not up to the task on a given day, it's probably a matter of uncooperative weather. Don't blame the trout because they are present and accounted for by scientific fisheries management.

In recent surveys, DEC electrofishing crews have estimated the upper Catt is home to approximately 600 adult brown and rainbow trout per mile. This part of the creek, from Springville upstream to Yorkshire, serves as the border between Erie and Cattaraugus counties. It is wider than you might think, between 20 and 30 feet across in most spots. The fishing where Elton Creek spills into the upper Catt, according to the DEC's Scott Cornett, is some of the best there is above the dam. Although foot-long specimens are much more common, you stand a decent chance of tangling with a fish half again or even twice that size when you try the current edges and undercuts in the water upstream and down from the meeting place of the upper Cattaraugus Creek and Elton Creek. Fishing for rainbows is excellent in this area. 'Bows of 10 to 14 inches are common, in the upper reaches of the Cattaraugus itself, and electrofishing studies show that browns of 16 to 19 inches are readily available, too, but angling traffic slows considerably in the summer. The big resident trout above Springville can turn on in a nano-second if a heavy summer shower cools the water a degree or two.

To find your way to this part of Cattaraugus Creek, use your dog-eared but still reliable copy of the DeLorme *New York Atlas & Gazetteer* to trace Route 16 where it heads north from the city of Olean in Cattaraugus County. Depending on your age, you will get the most from the DeLorme maps by keeping a magnifying glass in your glove compartment.

As a long first step, put your pinkie on the right page and use it to follow Route 16 north through Hinsdale, Cadiz, Franklinville and Machias, and keep going until you've passed Lime Lake. (The ice cream stand at the north end of the lake is the perfect place to regroup and rest a bit on a hot summer afternoon.) A few minutes after you've finished that medium-size Cotton Candy cone, you should see a nice looking stream on the right side of the road. It's the Lime Lake Outlet, a gorgeous little brook. We'll talk about it more a bit further along in this book, but for now, let's keep both eyes on the road, and keep heading north!

When you are just starting into the Village of Delevan, you'll notice that Main Street and Route 16 merge and sprout several side streets in a rather short time. The one you want is Mill Street. Turn left onto it, then drive up and over the hill. When you come to McKinstry Road, hang a right and drive north on that road for about 2 miles. Cross Stony Creek, which is a small and heavily posted stream, and look for Elton Road. The creek is about 25 feet wide in most spots, and the namesake creek will be flowing from right to left as you're heading north. After driving over the McKinstry Road bridge, make a sharp left and you will be able to see Cattaraugus Creek in a matter of seconds.

These streams and others which converge or narrowly miss converging in or near Delevan are mostly small in stature, yet always post high scores when their health and habitat are assessed by DEC work crews. I can't help but wonder how the reputations of streams like these will fare if—or is that "when"—dams, fish ladders and such have been removed, rebuilt or otherwise tailored to fulfill the needs and instincts of 10- to 15-pound steelhead. For now, at least, the wild trout that old-timers used to describe as "three to a pan," or about 10 or 12 inches when ready to cook, are holding their own.

Several of the most important tributaries of upper Cattaraugus Creek spring forth from the fertile ground in or near Delevan, in the northeast corner of Cattaraugus County, so let's take a peek at those waters, first. Then we might visit a couple of other streams that provide good fishing as tributaries of the Catt, and we definitely will single out the considerable opportunities in eastern and central Cattaraugus County, including Clear Creek near Arcade and Sandusky, the famed Ischua Creek and other tantalizing streams. After that, we might reel in our lines and shut down our computers so we can rest up for a few extra days of on-stream "scientific research."

CLEAR CREEK (ARCADE AREA)

RATING: ★★★★ (4 stars)

BEST TIME TO FISH: When other streams in northern Cattaraugus County are still muddy after a day or two of heavy rain.

BEST METHOD: Use your favorite bucktail or streamer pattern, hopefully one with a bit of flash and built-in action, and retrieve it across and down with fast line-strips.

I have a great fondness for streams named "Clear Creek," because such waters invariably clear up quickly after a drenching downpour. This natural tendency makes it very likely the stream will be eminently fishable hours or even days after other nearby trout waters are still the color of clay or black coffee. The best part is, the finned residents of any "Clear Creek" start their post-storm pig-outs almost immediately after heavy rain gives the water a tinge of color, but the bite will keep going long after mud plumes curtail the feeding just about everywhere else. Better yet, while other creeks in the neighborhood are too muddy to bode well for any method but bait fishing, the Clear Creeks in this world will be just transparent enough to make swinging a streamer fly or dead-drifting artificial nymphs wonderfully effective.

The Clear Creek you and I should be hustling to get to on our next day off is the one which flows northwest along Route 98 in Cattaraugus County and crosses into southern Wyoming County to join currents with the headwaters of Cattaraugus Creek. It is often referred to as Clear Creek (Arcade), for simplicity's sake. For sure, it helps to minimizes confusion with another Clear Creek which winds from near an

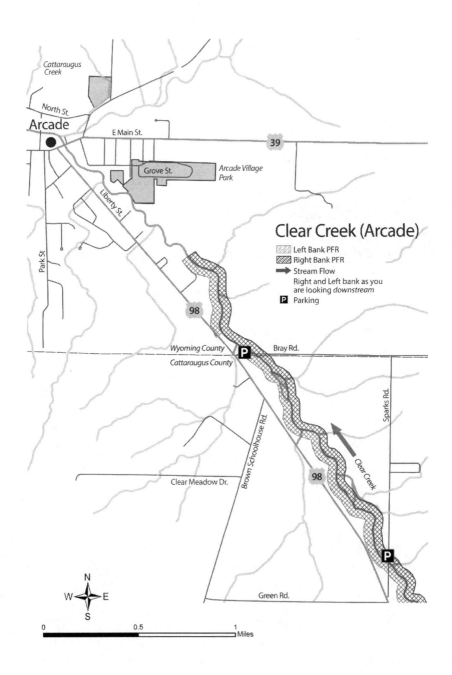

Cattaraugus
Creek

North St.

Arcade

E Main St.

39

Grove St.

Arcade Village
Park

Liberty St.

Park St

Clear Creek (Arcade)

Left Bank PFR
Right Bank PFR
Stream Flow
Right and Left bank as you
are looking *downstream*
P Parking

98

Wyoming County
Cattaraugus County

Bray Rd.

P

Sparks Rd.

Brown Schoolhouse Rd.

Clear Meadow Dr.

98

Clear Creek

P

Green Rd.

N
W   E
S

0   0.5   1
                        Miles

old ski center in Chautauqua County through the village of Ellington and across the Cattaraugus County border. That's how I will refer to it as we go forward.

While there's no need to count heads or sponsor a debate between the loyal supporters of one Clear Creek or the other, we can at least agree that Clear Creek Number Two—oops, I meant to say "Clear Creek (Arcade)"—is one hellacious trout stream. Among many other delightful characteristics, the one that stands out to me is its ease of access by traveling anglers. That part of Clear Creek which flows through Cattaraugus County has 4.5 miles of public fishing rights. A bit upstream from there, along parts of Route 98 at the hamlet of Freedom, you might encounter some of the disappearing water for which this region is well known. The tumbling currents drop underground and out of sight in this area during extremely dry weather, but don't worry; it always comes back, and icy-cold, at that.

A happy group of anglers and scientists is ready to survey Clear Creek near Arcade. The battery packs, dip nets and direct-current wands are used to gather data from the popular stream.

Clear Creek is about 20 feet wide in the vicinity of the county border areas described here, and it seldom gets any warmer than 68 or 70 degrees. Be forewarned, however, that the stream bed consists mainly of gravel and sand in this area, and the heavy rains that sometimes turn the trout on after a parched July and August can scour some spots to the point that they are unrecognizable. If you try fishing it after Labor Day, be prepared to fish very slowly and patiently, for you are, essentially, learning to fish the stream all over again.

A little extra effort will pay off with plenty of fish. During a stream survey in 2014, DEC workers calculated that Clear Creek (Arcade) was populated by 608 wild adult rainbows and 282 wild adult brown trout, per mile, in this out-of-the-way anglers' paradise. That may understate the possibilities, too, for a previous shocking expedition at the same sites in the summer of 2007 yielded significantly higher numbers of trout—including estimates of 586 wild, adult browns and 1,247 wild, adult rainbows per mile. Biologists suspect splitting the difference between these two sets of numbers might give a more accurate long-term picture of Clear Creek (Arcade).

A DEC worker sweeps a Clear Creek pool with an electrical current strong enough to stun trout and bring them to the surface.

You can find this stream by looking for Franklinville in your state *Atlas & Gazetteer*. From there, follow Route 16 north to the intersection with Route 98. Trace that road east for about 8 miles and make a sharp left turn which, after an additional 2 miles or so, will take you over the creek.

To zero in on a couple of very fine trout fishing opportunities north of Franklinville—which itself is on the famous Ischua Creek—go north (which is upstream) on Routes 16 and 98 for about 2 miles, then bear right. Go another 2 miles or so to where Kingsbury Road joins with Route 98. Go another 2½ miles on 98 to Farmersville. Take yet another left turn, which will lead you to Elton Creek, which is a better-than-average trout stream, itself. Alternately, continue north on Route 98 to Farmersville Station, Freedom and Sandusky, all of which provide good access to the upper and middle reaches of Clear Creek (Arcade) in Cattaraugus County.

DEC scientists say the stream's rainbows are mostly 6- to-8-inchers but sometimes stretch out to 11 inches. If you get a 13- or 14-incher in Clear Creek (Arcade), that's a feat comparable to netting a 20-inch brown elsewhere in western New York. Such specimens are present, in case you were wondering. Browns of 16 to 18 inches hide out effectively in some of the deeper pools and can be caught on a variety of lures (Mepps, Blue Fox and Panther Martin spinners among them), size 8 or 10 nymphs that are suggestive of the cranefly larvae that wash into the heavy currents after a heavy rain, and, of course, either garden worms or salted minnows.

I should warn newcomers to check the special regulations which apply to this particular Clear Creek. Here it goes: anglers can fish the creek (Arcade) from April 1–October 15 with any bait or lure that's permissible in the general statewide season. Within this calendar window, anglers can take up to five trout a day, with a nine-inch minimum creel length, but only two of your five trout can be more than 12 inches long. Then again, from Oct. 16–March 31, the fishery is catch-and-release only and bait is not allowed—just lures or flies, thank you.

LIME LAKE OUTLET

RATING: ★★★ (3 stars)

BEST TIME TO FISH: This is starting to sound a little repetitious, I know; but I still look forward to any rainfall that's big enough to roil trout-filled streams such as the Outlet.

BEST METHOD: You may out-fish me and my nightcrawlers with a streamer pattern that shows up in slightly muddier flows, like a black Wooly Bugger. But I doubt it, as worms are always on a trout's menu.

Lime Lake Outlet, when I first saw it, reminded me of a Madison County fishery that frustrated me for many years. The Chenango Canal, a dry fly fisherman's dream (or nightmare), crosses U.S. Route 20 just east south of Bouckville, and from there glides along until it spills over a petite dam and blends with more springs and side channels until it is considered part of Oriskany Creek. The canal is home to many medium-large brown trout, 15- to 18-inch beauties, and at first I was optimistic about fishing there. Well, the Canal's trout sent me packing routinely, and I began to think I would never connect with one of them. Then, one July morning, I said the heck with it. Instead of trying to creep along the bank until I got into a good casting spot, I splashed into the 15-feet-wide stream and stood stock still until all of the browns I scattered started to come back into their regular holding positions. I waited a good 10 minutes before casting again, and on the first try one of the first browns to return to its resting position sipped a floater pattern so that it would drift directly downstream. It worked so perfectly that one of the nervous casts stood the fly up on the surface and it vanished into a brown's mouth. It was only a 12-incher, but I couldn't have been any more pleased.

So it went, too, with the Lime Lake Outlet. Every cast, it seemed, either splashed down on the gravel bottom on the 6-foot-wide creek channel or caused a snarl in my leader or hang-up in the adjacent trees and shrubbery. Exasperated, I finally came up with a workable tactic which was based on my own Chenango Canal initiative. In this case, however, I was fishing with worms. It was just way too difficult to probe this part of the stream with a fly or even a weighted spinner

Lime Lake Outlet

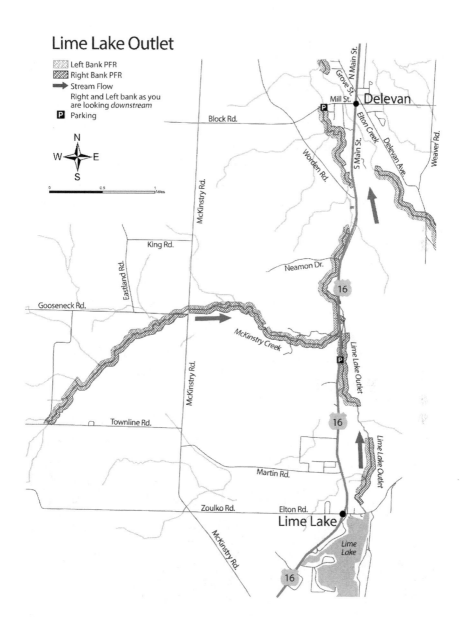

Left Bank PFR
Right Bank PFR
Stream Flow
Right and Left bank as you
are looking *downstream*
P Parking

N
W E
S

0   0.5   1 Miles

Block Rd.

Mill St. | Delevan

Grove St.
N Main St.
Elton Creek
S Main St.
Delevan Ave.
Weaver Rd.

Worden Rd.

McKinstry Rd.

King Rd.

Eastland Rd.

Neamon Dr.

16

Gooseneck Rd.

McKinstry Creek

Lime Lake Outlet

P

16

McKinstry Rd.

Townline Rd.

Lime Lake Outlet

Martin Rd.

Zoulko Rd.   Elton Rd.

Lime Lake

McKinstry Rd.

Lime
Lake

16

like a Rooster Tail or its kin. Because I could not cover the water using the old, reliable up-and-across cast, I waded in as deep as required to reach a trouty-looking spot and work my way downstream from there. I let the water calm down a bit before I raised the rod and began a careful retrieve—or merely lifted my nightcrawler off the bottom, it that's what it took. Though abundant, the Outlet fish are not very big. Lots of 8- to 10-inchers are waiting to be caught, when the water is up and a bit off color, but on some days, even anglers who consider themselves to be experts at the game will struggle to catch two or even one trout of any size. Browns and rainbows are abundant, but recent stream surveys have not produced any brook trout. Although he stopped shy of declaring the native char to be extirpated from Lime Lake Outlet, the DEC's Cornett said any brookies living in this place must have retreated into tiny tributaries, if they are present at all.

In addition to healthy populations of both browns and rainbows, this creek has another big plus in its favor, namely, plenty of public access. My favorite signs, the yellow ones with green messages on them, are hung

The author wades the icy currents of Lime Lake Outlet, which flows north from the small lake through the village of Delevan. It holds many 8- to 12-inch brown trout and plenty of wild rainbows, too.

up in can't-miss-'em trees and fence posts. They are prominently located along 4.4 miles of the outlet. Only about a half mile of the stream—or about 10 percent of its total length—is *not* open to fishing. How many trout streams have you ever encountered that are as accessible as this one?

Lime Lake Outlet, north of the lake, bubbles and swirls near, along and under Route 16, which winds northward from Olean to Delevan. Most of the journey takes anglers along Ischua Creek, which we will cover in depth a few pages ahead.

MCKINSTRY CREEK

RATING: ★★★ (3 stars)

BEST TIME TO FISH: Get to this one just as the rain is starting to fall, if you can. It muddies up quickly and won't clear as fast as some of its neighbor creeks.

BEST METHOD: The bait-fishers have an advantage in McKinstry Creek, but anyone who knows how to rig a three-fly "cast" of wet flies can stir up some good size trout with a slow hand-twist retrieve.

Come to think of it, you might out-do yourself by stirring up some hard-fighting trout with a slightly faster retrieve than usual. Wild browns, especially, but also wild rainbows and occasional wild brookies lurk under cover in this compact five-mile-long stream. When the rains are on the way, they appear to know it, and they quickly respond to the falling barometer by moving out quietly to attack their next meal. That menu often includes the same wandering garden worms, cranefly larvae, crickets and grasshoppers that were lying close to the bank before the current line of showers got our hearts racing.

If you are a religious person, be sure to thank the powers above for convincing landowners on the banks of McKinstry Creek to make 4.2 miles of the creek (out of about 5 miles, total) available to anglers. At times, fishermen might feel hemmed in by the dense willows and rip-rap installed here and there by the state Department of Transportation to keep erosion to a minimum. However, the medium- and old-growth woodlands and overgrown fields in other places along the creek are relatively easy to fish even with 8- to 10-foot fly rods.

McKinstry Creek is another good stream in Delevan, and typically holds its own through drought conditions.

McKinstry Creek isn't hard to find. Use Olean as a ball-marker, so to speak. On your regional map, whether it's on paper or down-loaded to a desktop computer, you will wish to begin your personal introduction to the creek by following Route 16 north, past the aforementioned upper end of Lime Lake Outlet. Next, drive into the village of Delevan, go left on Mill Street, then over the bridge and left again onto McKinstry Road. Drive about a mile and three-quarters to a crossing of the stream.

ISCHUA CREEK

RATING: ★★★★ (4 stars)
BEST TIME TO FISH: The merry, merry month of mayflies.
BEST METHOD: Because the middle and upper thirds of Ischua Creek are home to a wide variety of mayfly and caddis hatches in May, any fly-fisher will want to get in on the fun.

Most years, the Hendricksons are the first mayflies of hatch-matching consequence on the calendars of experienced Ischua Creek anglers. The

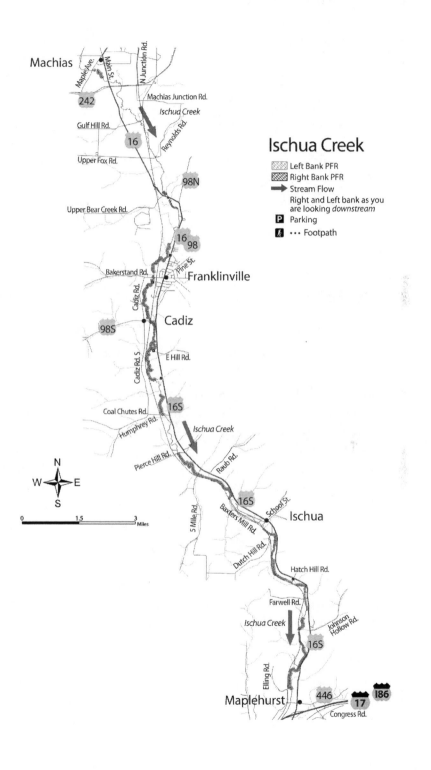

Ischua Creek

Machias

242

Maple Ave.

Main St.

N Junction Rd.

Machias Junction Rd.

Ischua Creek

Gulf Hill Rd.

16

Reynolds Rd.

Upper Fox Rd.

98N

Upper Bear Creek Rd.

16 98

Pine St.

Bakerstand Rd.

Franklinville

Cadiz Rd.

Cadiz

98S

Cadiz Rd. S

E Hill Rd.

Coal Chutes Rd.

16S

Humphrey Rd.

Ischua Creek

Pierce Hill Rd.

Raub Rd.

5 Mile Rd.

16S

Baxters Mill Rd.

School St.

Ischua

Dutch Hill Rd.

Hatch Hill Rd.

Farwell Rd.

Ischua Creek

Johnson Hollow Rd.

16S

Elling Rd.

446

17 186

Maplehurst

Congress Rd.

Legend:
- Left Bank PFR
- Right Bank PFR
- Stream Flow
- Right and Left bank as you are looking *downstream*
- P Parking
- ... Footpath

N
W E
S

0   1.5   3
Miles

plump, pinkish size 12 or 14 duns can show up as early as the last couple days of April if the water is low and the weather has been on the mild side. However, the emergence is more likely to debut during the first week of May, under normal weather and water conditions. Once the Hendricksons are officially "on," anglers will notify each other via email or cell phone, and the ritual intensifies as other species of aquatic insects take their turns at popping through the creek's smooth surface. Following the Hendricksons in a predictable sequence are the March Browns, Blue-winged Olives, and the elusive Green Drakes. The drakes make a strong impression most years, but every now and then the sizes 8 and 10 mayflies go A.W.O.L. and rumors of their demise spread up and down the Ischua valley. However, the fly-fishing doomsayers tend to forget a few things. First, the Green Drake hatch on the Ischua, as on countless other streams, seldom lasts more than a week or so. This means it is almost always a "get 'em while they're hot" event. Second, if the weather has been unseasonably warm, the long-anticipated evening hatch might take place entirely after dark. As a result, the party easily could come and go without anyone knowing it happened. A third possibility, one that has haunted drake chasers since fly-fishing has existed, is a sparse emergence of Green Drake duns during daylight hours, followed by dense, night-long swarms of drake spinners, or "Coffin Flies."

Coffin flies, which have chalky white abdomens and speckled black wings, mate in mid-air above the water, jettison their fertilized eggs, and fall, one by one, on the stream surface, whether the splashdown occurs on Ischua Creek or the West Branch of the Ausable River near Lake Placid. The bite-size bugs are utterly helpless upon landing, and some of the larger trout in Ischua Creek, bruisers measuring 18–22 inches long, will come topside to gorge on flies that are easy pickings. You say you've tried to get in on this feeding frenzy for years, without success? Here's what you can do to make up for lost time on the water. These tips will help anyone deal with the drakes, and that applies to streams other than Ischua Creek, too.

My first piece of advice is to widen your circle of friends to include a local angler or even a non-local "regular" on Ischua Creek pools. Make sure they keep close track of the hatches on your targeted streams.

Shady bridge crossings both north and south of Franklinville offer excellent fishing with bait or lure early in the trout season.

Pester these new friends as D-Day ("Drake Day," of course) is getting close. Your goal is to get there in time to see the first duns of the year, and then stick around for the final Coffin Fly, too. Second, when you think you have arrived at a good time, for a change, resolve to make the most of the opportunity by staying on the water until well after sundown. Third, make sure your last-minute preparations include tying a 30-inch length of 4X or 5X monofilament tippet to your leader. Work a bit of floatant into the last 10 or 15 feet of your fly line, while you are at it; and remind yourself to double-check all of your knots, before it's too dark to see. Fourth, before the sun drops below the Allegany mountain peaks, do some peeking, yourself. You should look skyward, for very large mayfly spinners silhouetted against the sky. White abdomens that resemble inch-long pieces of pipe cleaners are what you hope to see. As they plop down onto the water, some of the coffin flies may drift unmolested, at first, but the more large mayflies you see, the more trout will line up for their share.

If you fail to hook a couple of nice trout on mega mayflies in May, you can be confident of getting some hatch-matching do-overs in June and even during the dog days of summer on the Ischua. The summer hatches in Western New York in general and especially in the spring-fed sections on the Ischua, around Cadiz and Franklinville, are profuse. After the large, marquee mayflies have finished until next year, one can pass the time through June, July and keep going through late September, if desired. There will be plenty of bugs about, but with a couple of exceptions, their emergences tend to be sporadic. The hatches that shine during the summer fishing challenges include a smorgasbord of tiny, olive-bodied flies that are mimicked by floating flies spun on size 20 hooks, succeeded by the even more abundant "Tricos," little black and white mayflies that are matched on 22s , 24s or size 26 patterns. There are so many little olives hatching on rainy mornings during July, August and September that some anglers tend to overlook the astonishing numbers of Tricos that swarm over gentle riffles when water temperatures hit 68 degrees or so. Because the Tricos and olives, combined, are so abundant between them, fly fishers should take care to pick imitations which are dead ringers for the real thing, and size 6X or 7X leader tippets aren't too small. For me, the most difficult aspect of these summer hatches, on Ischua Creek or elsewhere, is finding a way to poke my tippet through the hook eye of a suitable dry fly!

Once widely considered to be among New York's top trout waters, Ischua Creek upstream and down from the village of Franklinville has lost some of its fan base over the years. Yet it still holds plenty of promise for serious brown-trout seekers. Sitting in a wide valley, it takes a 40-mile ride from its origins near Lime Lake, and it changes character almost continuously as it alternately hurries or pokes along on its way south. So lazy and sinuous does it appear, initially, that when an angler starts to explore the creek, he is astonished by its slow pace. One can be excused for thinking that Ischua Creek is not a trout stream, at all—but it is, and a darned good one, too. Technically, Ischua Creek ceases to be when it joins Oil Creek at the junction near Routes 16 and U.S. Route 86. Together, the merged creeks are known as Olean Creek.

I note these natural happenings so that readers will have a better understanding of why their 6-pound-test leaders sometimes go limp without apparent warning, and also why giant but rarely seen fish roll at the surface of deep, mysterious pools in Ischua Creek and the waters to which it is linked. For even though this river valley north of Olean and Allegany is justly known for putting 20-inch brown trout on anglers' sharp hooks, its local population of fish is dominated, more often than not, by northern pike and muskellunge. Some of these river monsters are very well-proportioned, or positively fearsome.

My most recent visit to the Ischua Creek valley, in July of 2016, was a dud, trout-wise, mainly because the stream was sorely impacted by a drought-like weather pattern. We had to put up with extremely low water, big buildups of algae in the eddies and backwaters, fish out-migrating from risky hiding places, and so forth. My wife, Chickie, and I were enthused when we started fishing, but we were frankly discouraged at the conclusion of our first day on the creek. On the second day of the trip, we endured more poor fishing, but at least stayed alert, after sharing the water with several kayakers. The leader of the group slowed down as they approached and then slipped under the Pierce Hill Road bridge.

"A friend of mine caught a 42-inch northern pike right *there*," the 20-something lad said, meanwhile pointing at the spot with paddle. "On the first day of pike season, too."

That pool did not draw a single strike that morning for the kayakers or us, either, in case you were wondering.

Ischua Creek's better trout habitat is perhaps 10 to 20 miles upstream from its junction with Oil Creek, but it has more trout, including both stocked and wild fish, than its Plain Jane looks might indicate. A bit more than 17 miles of this flat, low-gradient stream has public fishing signs overlooking the water. About 15 miles of Ischua Creek are stocked by DEC hatchery crews with occasional assistance from angler volunteers and state fisheries biologists or technicians. Research has proven, with little room for doubt, that pre-season stocking truck runs are largely a waste of time in this watershed—and probably in quite a few others in western New York, too. The water is simply too cold and muddy. As a result of these scientific inquiries, the DEC has recently stocked Region 9 creeks with hatchery browns (and a smaller output of brook trout) starting in April and ending around the third week of May.

The stocked areas, for the most part, are marked by signs that clearly denote "public fishing rights" or "angler foot path" locations pointed toward the stream corridor which is paralleled by Route 16.

The upper Cattaraugus Creek near Sardinia and its not-so-small tributaries are extremely popular with trout fishermen living in the Buffalo-Niagara Falls area.

Lately, the DEC Region 9 fisheries unit has fine-tuned stocking quotas for Ischua Creek. Hatchery transplants now include annual releases in the stream of 4,725 yearling brown trout, 1,500 of the state's two-year-old browns, plus 3,325 state-reared brook trout that usually measure approximately 8 to 10 inches long. Too bad that state studies indicate only a tiny percentage of stockers hold over in the creek between fishing seasons. In Ischua Creek, the standing crop of wild or stocked brown trout—more wild ones than hatchery grads, actually— amounts to around 100 adults per mile. By western New York standards, that's a fair number of trout, but nothing to get excited about. The main problem is not warm summer temperatures. Sink a stream thermometer in the water between Franklinville and Cadiz and you will seldom get a reading higher than 70 degrees. Not coincidentally, this four- or five-mile stretch of the creek is one of the likelier places in the creek to connect with a 20-incher.

When you look at regional data without preconceptions, the unavoidable conclusion is that Ischua Creek's sport fishery depends heavily on the output from DEC hatcheries. The same can be said, however, for the trout fishing encountered in many other New York waters. Just to emphasize this point, I would encourage readers to consider their own experiences on the Beaverkill in the Catskills, the West Branch of the Ausable in the Adirondacks and West Canada Creek in central New York, to name just three examples of popular fisheries which owe at least a significant share of their angling reputations to hatchery-born trout.

Having acknowledged the poor medium-size carry-over population noted in Ischua Creek in recent years, many anglers remain convinced that Ischua Creek could be a much better fishery than it is. Fishermen could help the cause, the stream's advocates insist, by asking Department of Environmental Conservation experts in Albany to take a long, hard look at the sluggish currents and loose silt that complicate the annual spawning runs in Ischua Creek. The mix of mud and gravel doesn't stand up very well during years marked by heavy downpours and subsequent flooding. The Ischua, which can run extremely high one summer and have a gaunt, skeletal appearance a year later, might also be a prime candidate for the installation of "permanent" stream-improvement devices, such as wood-and-wire cribbing, plunge pools and boulder "necklaces" that would cause the creek's currents to scour deep pools where today there are none. That's what staunch trout-fishers argue, anyway, but few anglers volunteer to purchase a state-wide habitat and access stamp or make any other financial sacrifice to improve the health of fading trout fisheries.

MANSFIELD CREEK

RATING: ★★★★ (4 stars)

BEST TIME: Because Mansfield Creek flows over a substrate of clay for much of its length and tends to turn muddy sooner than most western New York streams, the day after a heavy rain storm can be very productive. Hit other area creeks the day of the downpour and save Mansfield itself for the following day.

BEST METHOD: If you have the patience to fish them properly, small Rapala-type stickbaits with trout paint jobs and Panther Martins with yellow or black shanks and silver- or gold-finish spinner blades will get you lots of fish in that muddy water.

Ellicottville is known for the Holiday Valley resort and great downhill and cross-country skiing. Yet any angler who tucks a combo fly-spin rod in his car trunk just in case unexpectedly mild weather leaves the slopes in poor shape will be glad he (or she) kept the fishing gear handy. Mansfield Creek is possibly the best of several prominent trout streams north of Salamanca. To find it on your DeLorme *Atlas* or some other detailed New York topographical map, look for the village of Orchard Park (home of the Buffalo Bills football stadium), and just to its west, you'll see the intersection of Route 20A and Route 219. Follow Route 219 south for about 20 miles to Springville. Keep going south on Route 219 but keep an eye out for County Route 13, also known as Maples Road. It's a right hand turn, and easy to miss, but in this instance, if you've come to Ellicottville, you have gone too far south and need to turn around. As you're driving north out of Ellicottville, you will see Poverty Hill Road on the right. Bear left and proceed on Route 13 to Orlando and then to Maples Road. In this area Mansfield Creek is about 15 feet across, but it averages around 20 feet wide—with some decent dry fly pools up to 30 feet across, as it approaches its junction with the South Branch of Cattaraugus Creek.

About 2.4 miles of Mansfield Creek are stocked with 700 yearling and two-year-old brown trout, annually. The stocked section, which ends at Eddyville Corners, is paralleled by Route 13 and Maples Road. Along with hatchery fish, this stretch holds some wild ones, including a fair number of 12- to 15-inch browns, but if you continue driving along Hinman Road, more and more wild browns and some rainbows, too, can be found in this 8-mile-long stream. In 2013, an electrofishing crew estimated the population of wild trout in upper Mansfield Creek at approximately 486 adult wild browns and 475 adult wild rainbows per mile. One of the captured browns was a 20-incher. More important for anglers, in the long run, was the discovery of several strong year-classes of trout in the creek. As a veteran trout biologist explained it to me back in the 1970s, a stream that holds several strong year-classes of wild trout is healthier, on the whole, than one which has a few very large trout per mile but a low-density population of small and medium-size fish. On that level, the Mansfield Creek trout are pretty impressive.

Of the total number of adult brownies which were systematically collected, examined and released during the 2013 survey, 64 per mile were greater than 10 inches long, 45 per mile were longer than 12 inches and 17 per mile were longer than 14 inches. As to the wild rainbows in Mansfield Creek, the electro-shockers reported handling 475 adult 'bows during the 2013 expedition. Clearly, the rainbows introduced to the neighborhood more than a decade earlier had more than held their own against predators, anglers, severe weather and other dangers.

The DEC's recent summer excursions in Mansfield Creek produced data that suggested this stream is one that might benefit by a reduction in stocking quotas or even doing away with any stocking-truck visits at all in the near future.

Meanwhile, fishermen in the Southern Tier should give this lightly pressured stream a serious try. Although Mansfield Creek can be challenging to fish at times, and is doubly difficult for anybody who has scant knowledge of how rising, muddy water impacts trout behavior, the stream has many positive aspects, starting with nearly 8 miles of public access. Some of the best fishing sections in the creek are plainly visible along Route 13 and Hinman Hollow Road.

Access to Mansfield Creek is excellent. About 6.3 miles of the creek has public-fishing signs along its banks, and first-time visitors need not worry about having to slug their way to the water. The creek is guarded in some spots by dense willows, but for the most part it is easy to approach and can be fished effectively with fly rod and reel. The stream has fair to good mayfly and caddis populations and plenty of room to employ straight-line and roll-casting tactics.

I wasn't kidding when I suggested tucking a fishing rod in your car in case your mid-winter ski trip in Cattaraugus County is jeopardized by rainy weather or a sudden thaw. Mansfield Creek is managed for year-round fishing, and there are many days between Thanksgiving and Easter Sunday when it could be worth fishing. From October 16 through March 31 the creek is subject to catch and release regulations, meaning you can catch all the trout you want, but each must be released in good condition. Only artificial lures or flies may be used. From April 1–October 15, the regular statewide trout-season dates, there is no minimum size limit on trout in the creek. During this time, known as "the regular season" by most New York anglers, you can keep five a day if you wish, but only two of the five can exceed 12 inches in length.

Don't be shocked if you run into one or two other anglers when you try to hurry spring a bit. Although angler traffic along Mansfield Creek and many other Western New York trout waters is light most of the year, there are always a few fanatics out there who simply can't pass up the slightest chance to catch a fat trout or two; and I have met quite a few—not counting myself—who have hooked and landed trout while stream-fishing in every month of the year.

ELTON CREEK

RATING: ★★★ (3 stars)
BEST TIME: After a good, all-day soaker in the summer, Elton Creek can serve up some fine fishing.
BEST METHOD: Live bait, if you like it; in-line spinners if you don't.

Many inexperienced trout anglers are bewildered when they visit a stream which changes drastically from its headwaters to its mouth, but in fact, that's a trait shared by most of our better fisheries. Elton Creek is a good example. Born in northwestern Allegany County, this medium-size stream (about 20 miles long and 30-feet across after it crosses the Cattaraugus County border) is seriously harmed by beaver activity in its upper reaches. The mid-section of the creek is a different story, as the silt generated by dam-building settles out of the water column in and below the village of Elton. Unfortunately, the creek warms up again by the time it reaches the village of Delevan.

DEC fisheries unit employees make the most of Elton Creek's habitat by stocking 200 or so yearling browns immediately upstream from Mud Lake in Farmersville. A notably larger allocation of browns, about 2,300 yearlings and 200 two-year-olds, are released at bridge crossings in the 4.2 miles of water upstream from the junction of Elton Creek and Route 16 in Delevan. The trout stocked in this part of the watershed are supplemented by a rather modest population of wild trout, estimated at 133 adult browns and 49 adult rainbows per mile during a 2013 survey.

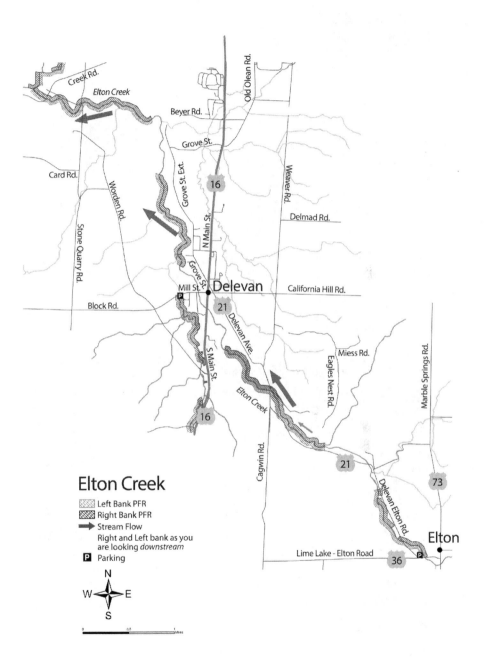

Creek Rd.

Elton Creek

Beyer Rd.

Old Olean Rd.

Grove St.

Card Rd.

Worden Rd.

Grove St. Ext.

16

Weaver Rd.

Delmad Rd.

Stone Quarry Rd.

N Main St.

Grove St.

Mill St.   Delevan

California Hill Rd.

Block Rd.

P

21

S Main St.

Delevan Ave.

Miess Rd.

Eagles Nest Rd.

Marble Springs Rd.

16

Elton Creek

Cagwin Rd.

21

73

Delevan Elton Rd.

Elton Creek

Left Bank PFR
Right Bank PFR
Stream Flow
Right and Left bank as you
are looking *downstream*
P Parking

N
W   E
S

0   0.5   1
                        Miles

Lime Lake - Elton Road

36

P

Elton

Elton Creek near Sardinia is one of many streams in the Cattaraugus Creek watershed which have good fishing for brown trout—wild, stocked, or both.

Fishing is much better from Delevan upstream along Route 21 to the village of Elton. There, biologists estimated the trout population in 2013 at approximately 183 adult browns and an eye-popping 820 adult rainbows, per mile in both instances. Region 9 trout-water expert, Mr. Cornett, touts this part of Elton Creek as a consistent producer of big, wild browns, including some in the 16- to 19-inch category. Such fish are caught on a fairly consistent basis by anglers who know how to fish in rising, off-colored stream, Cornett said.

As you might have guessed already, colder water accounts for the sharp rise in catch rates between Delevan and Elton. Shady cover and intermittent spring seeps do the trick for the trout.

Elton Creek, though born in the northwest corner of Allegany County, comes into its own in neighboring Cattaraugus County. Its best stretches, in and around the village of Elton, flow north along Route 21. Avoid the beaver dams as much as possible, because they are full of silt and frequently too warm to support trout through the summer.

ELM CREEK

RATING: ★★★★ (4 stars)

BEST TIME: Late April, when the trout are starting to hit all day long and the stream is in nearly perfect condition more days than not.

BEST METHOD: Fly-fishers should love this place. But a small, white Glo Bug will likely out-fish more traditional patterns in this setting, a couple of casts from the state's Randolph Fish Hatchery. Darned if I know why, but this salmon-egg imitation almost always works in clear, cold, challenging spots like Randolph.

Elm Creek, located near the hatchery but not precisely within its boundaries, is popular among anglers who live close by it in northern Cattaraugus County, and withstands moderate fishing pressure through May and June in most years. The stream, which flows in a generally southward direction through the village of Randolph, has only about 3 miles of fishable water, and is less than 20 feet wide in most places. If that strikes you as being a small stream, well, think again, for Elm Creek is crammed with trout. According to DEC reports, the creek's

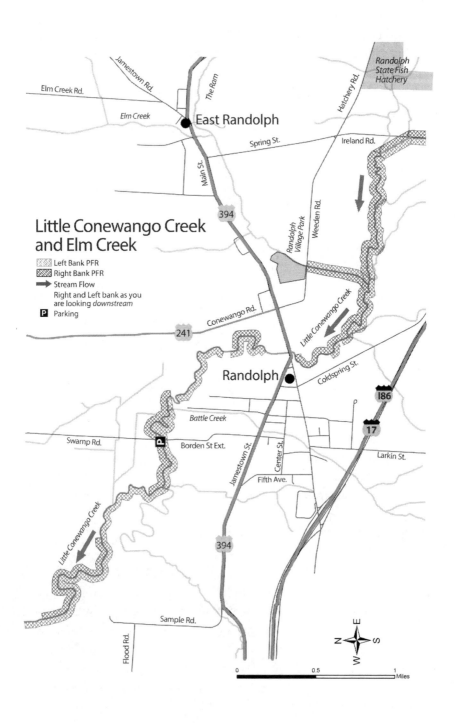

Little Conewango Creek
and Elm Creek

Left Bank PFR
Right Bank PFR
Stream Flow
Right and Left bank as you
are looking *downstream*
P Parking

East Randolph

Randolph

Elm Creek Rd.
Jamestown Rd.
The Ram
Elm Creek
Randolph
State Fish
Hatchery
Hatchery Rd.
Spring St.
Ireland Rd.
Main St.
394
Weeden Rd.
Randolph
Village Park
Conewango Rd.
241
Little Conewango Creek
Coldspring St.
186
17
Battle Creek
Swamp Rd.
Borden St Ext.
Jamestown St.
Center St.
Larkin St.
Fifth Ave.
Little Conewango Creek
394
Sample Rd.
Flood Rd.

0   0.5   1
Miles

N
E
W
S

population of browns was estimated at 927 wild adults per mile, as of the year 2013. These browns are all grown-up already or are soon to be grown, mind you. Scott Cornett's files of electrofishing data indicate the creek's residents include "a dense population of browns." These wild beauties appear to average perhaps 10 to 12 inches long, but the stream holds a good number of 16- to 18-inchers, too, along with numerous young of the year hatchlings and lots of 5- to 9 inchers.

Access to Elm Creek is not notably difficult, although you may need to ask private property owners for permission to wet a line here and there. The creek flows at a moderate speed from its headwaters off Elm Creek Road in East Randolph to its junction with Little Conewango Creek in Randolph. The town park on Weeden Road is well worth trying, even on those sweltering August days when few anglers are confident of their prospects on the Elm. A small feeder brook known as Mill Creek or "the Ram," merits some attention here, as well. The Ram does not usually hold large numbers of trout, but it has been known to hide some browns that stretched almost the full length of DEC measuring boards in recent stream surveys.

To find Elm Creek, first look on your map for Jamestown, which is approximately 15 miles west of Randolph. Take U.S. Route 86 (the Southern Tier Expressway) from Jamestown to the Randolph exit. Once on the creek, you will find hip boots adequate for most pools. The background consists primarily of first and second-growth forests—along with a couple of farm fields and plenty of backyards, too. Trout are fairly abundant throughout Elm Creek, from its mouth upstream to the headwaters in East Randolph.

OTHER CATTARAUGUS COUNTY TROUT STREAMS

Along with the top-notch waters covered in the preceding pages, Cattaraugus County has at least a dozen additional streams which are home to browns, rainbows or brookies—stocked, wild or both. And that assessment of the county's trout fishing doesn't include the beautiful, backwoods rivulets that course through the 65,000-acre Allegany State Park. The publisher and I agree that the park is so special it deserves a chapter of its own, and will get it, a few pages farther along. Before we get around to that chore, however, let me give an angler's shout-out to some of the other Cattaraugus County streams that readers might want to add to their personal fishing vests, roomy willow creels, or other tote bags.

As I organized this chapter, I was struck by how many of the smaller streams in the county could have been considered 3-, 4-, or even 5-star waters in any given year. If 2016 was a tough year for New York trout fishing in general, and it definitely was, I felt confident that many of the creeks and brooks which virtually receded into Mother Earth during long months without significant rainfall would come back in the next year or two. Let us hope so, anyway!

The streams in DEC Region 9 which deserve serious attention from the angling public when things get back to normal include **Fenton Creek**, also known as Mud Creek. This underrated stream is about 6 miles long, with a width of about 15 feet and pools averaging three to five feet. It meanders through the community of Leon, off Route 62. The upper half of the creek has a respectable population of adult wild browns—about 439 of them per mile—along with a modest number of adult wild rainbows. The downstream half of the creek is very flat and slow-flowing. As there are no public fishing rights on Fenton Creek, you should plan on getting permission from the landowners, including several Amish farmers.

Another good one is **Forks Creek**. Located north of Salamanca along Route 98 above and below the hamlet of Sugartown, the Forks is an early-season stream that warms up quickly and has no public access. Is it worth your while to knock on some doors for the purpose of gaining access? Well, ask DEC biologists whose survey of the creek in 2013 netted a 25½-inch brown, one of the biggest fish ever collected during a Western New York electrofishing study. Unfortunately, only 12 other wild browns were captured in the 2013 fish hunt, which covered more than 2,000 linear feet of the Forks. But you can bet the survey crews didn't catch them all.

When you are in this neighborhood, consider the **Southwest Branch of Cattaraugus Creek**. It is a 15-foot wide stream, on average, and has fairly good instream and overhead cover, but its tendency to warm into the 70s by late May or so justifies its reputation as a simple put-and-take fishery. It's stocked near East Otto, which is a couple of thrown stones from Mansfield Creek, at a rate of about 1,200 yearling browns each season. About 1.8 miles of the South Branch are posted as Public Fishing areas, but don't expect much better than mediocre action.

Still more trout fishing is available at **Connoisarauley Creek**, which flows through a small gorge downstream of Connoisarauley Road in the town of East Otto. Intermittently posted, it holds mostly stocked and wild browns but also attracts a small run of steelhead that ends below an impassable falls.

Several remote brooks that hold brown and/or native brook trout are worth a serious look when you're hunting for new places to fish in Cattaraugus County. **Guernsey Run**, for example, has a few brook trout and more browns—most of them wild—in the town of South Valley, off Guernsey Hollow. Unfortunately, the Run is one of many streams in the county that warm up fast, forcing most of its trout to seek refuge in spring holes or tiny tributaries before summer shows up. Another small but tempting stream is **Johnson Creek**, a feeder of Ischua Creek that can be seen on your right about a mile and a quarter north of Franklinville, near the intersection of Routes 16 and 98. Expect all the trout you encounter here to be browns. Most are under 8 inches long, but every so often you might get a 12-incher that has come up from Ischua Creek to take refuge from the summer heat.

If you don't cringe at the thought of catching a muskellunge, add **Little Conewango Creek** to your list of places to try out when you're on your way to or from the streams other fishermen forget about. It's most abundant game fish are stocked browns that sometimes hold over from season to season. Muskies are improbable but not impossible, especially in the muddy lower end of the creek, but the state didn't hang its public fishing signs along 8 miles of banks for nothing. You can find the Little Conewango easily enough by taking U.S. 86 to the Randolph exit and then driving east on Route 394 (Main Street) through town. It doesn't look nor fish as well as Elm Creek, but is worth a quick visit when the latter stream is crowded or temporarily not to your liking.

CHAPTER THREE

Streams of Allegany State Park

While I am not all-powerful, nor all-knowing or all-anything, I certainly can tell when I am sharing a stream with a fellow brook-trout aficionado. One definite tip-off is the frequency of strikes, landings and gentle releases. Clearly, the fellow knows his stuff, and he rigs, casts and sets his hooks with the delicate precision of a surgeon. The way this angler confidently wades and clambers over and around rotting tree trunks and wet, slippery boulders, yet rarely takes a serious tumble when exploring a small stream, is another clue. Most telling, however, is the absence of any trash in this fisherman's wake. The bright, clean moss on the upstream trail suggests that such a gentle soul doesn't leave behind even a single footprint when he is checking up on the health of a pretty stream. Now a middle-aged man, he so loves *Salvelinus fontinalis* that he has spent a good share of his life learning everything he can about brook trout and the fragile habitats where they live. It is a difficult mission he has chosen, at the very least, and there are days when he wonders whether the "natives," or people like himself, will be first to vanish from American waters.

In fact, if you ask Scott Cornett what sort of trout fishing he loves best, the Department of Environmental Conservation's undisputed trout maven in western New York might surprise you with his answer. Oh, he could lead you on a bit of a goose chase, and admit to being a big fan of big fish; but he would eventually steer the conversation back to the quaking bogs, beaver dams and tag alder jungles of Allegany State Park, where New York's native char, also known as the brook trout, is angling royalty. Obviously, Cornett loves his work, even the part where he and his colleagues step aside and let Mother Nature do the heavy-duty stuff.

The summer of 2016 challenged trout and angler to survive, let alone thrive. Although the tiny waters that duck under culverts and curl around fallen timber throughout the 65,000-acre state park were shrunken by drought that year, Cornett felt the fish would make a strong comeback before many more weeks passed. That's what brook trout do. They persist, and often in places where just hanging on is itself a spectacular achievement. They survive, somehow, in places where cold water is a priceless commodity, yet do not do much better in spring creeks that could afford to pass the good stuff around. They wax fat in streams that are stuffed with their species, and sometimes outfight the more voracious browns and rainbows that challenge them for the best feeding runs and the ideal spawning sites in trout waters everywhere. Maybe the best way to salute them is to admit, up front, that brook trout are where you find them, and they will continue to cling to tried-and-true hiding places until fish that are bigger, tougher and more tolerant of pollution and other problems can merely chase the natives away.

Not long ago my wife and I were driving rather aimlessly in the southwest corner of New York. It was the next-to-last day of a short vacation and we had mixed feelings about heading home so soon, because a line of heavy thunderstorms was brewing to the west, and the local trout fishing was likely to improve in the short run. Unfortunately, we couldn't stick around for long, but we had a couple of trout rods handy in the back of our SUV.

Our explorations that afternoon led us to the main drag of a very small community, the name of which I am unwilling to reveal, for reasons that any trout fisher would understand. Rain was spattering on the windshield when I first noticed the stream that slipped under town's main street bridge. It couldn't have been more than 15 feet across, and one of the pools we could see was smooth-topped and just slightly roiled by the most recent showers. Was it worth fishing, I wondered? We stopped for a fill-up at a convenience store and asked whether the spot was fishable. The proprietor of the store said folks gave it a try, now and then, and his observation that there were no "posted" signs along the brook was all the extra encouragement I needed. Even as the rain started to come down, I was rigging my longest rod, an 11-footer—with a single-action fly reel that was spooled with 4-pound mono. I figured the rain would add color to the water and thereby bring resident fish, if any, to form a chow line full of nightcrawlers and other trout snacks before too many minutes had passed.

My wife, who is almost always wiser than me, decided to take shelter before the contents of the black clouds in the west gave the little community a thorough soaking. She opted to curl up in the front passenger seat of the car with a new book. I, on the other hand, hustled down the road to get a better look at the same pool that had caught our attention just a few minutes earlier. The brook was clear at the margins but its depths were gloomy and mysterious, and I wondered if the rest of the stream was as deep as this hole seemed to be. My initial estimate of a hole that could not be safely waded looked to be on the money. I realized, as I lobbed a 'crawler upstream and across the spot, that I had not thought to ask our friendly convenience store boss what species of fish lived here. Nor had I inquired whether I might do any harm or stir bad feelings by walking across the soaked but recently manicured lawn that bordered the pool. Such vague worries disappeared in an instant, as my first cast resulted in a sharp tug and I lifted a 5-inch brook trout from the water. Another, slightly larger native came next, and then something much heavier and stronger managed to hook itself on my rig. The fish rolled stubbornly near the bottom of the creek, shaking its head fiercely, and I bent my rod over double while the obvious ruler of this watery treasure chest pulled back as hard as it could. *A brown trout? What about a rainbow?*

Amazingly, the trout that flopped on that green lawn a few moments later was a brookie, a wild one of truly impressive proportions. It was exactly 15 inches long, undoubtedly stream-bred and beautifully sprayed with haloed spots and, on its dorsal surface, gorgeous but random vermiculations. The rose-colored fins were trimmed with black and white on the edges. It was a perfect match for another 15-incher, which according to my fishing diaries had been removed from a central

New York meadow brook and tenderly placed in my wicker creel back in 1981. In other words, it was either the biggest wild brook trout I had ever landed, or the next-largest. Since two such fish sound better than one, I declared a tie. Wouldn't you?

Such brook trout—or char, if you prefer scientific precision in these matters—are seldom encountered in New York except in certain Adirondack ponds, and most of those stunning specimens spent time in hatcheries before being transplanted to more remote places. The memory of them is replayed over and over in the minds of the fishermen who are lucky enough to make their acquaintance.

In these times, I doubt there are more than a handful of western New York streams capable of growing a 15-inch native, but many waters in the region support modest numbers of wild brookies. Allegany State Park stands out because it is a large tract of land with dozens of cold, small- to medium-size trout streams coursing through its gullies and glades.

Each April, state tankers seed several of the park's streams with hatchery-reared brown trout, and wild browns are also found in a few

Many of the more than two dozen small trout waters in Allegany State Park beg to be fished with a wide variety of lures, bait and flies.

park waters. However, the large majority of creeks and brooks in the park are populated entirely with natives. Most of these creatures are four- to seven-inch sprites, but brook trout of 8 or 9 inches in length are not unusual. The DEC does not stock any brook trout inside the state park out of concerns about harmful interbreeding.

Those brookies have other worries, too. Come spring, and the streams are populated not only by other wild and stocked browns, but also herons, kingfishers and other avian predators. Mink and the occasional river otter don't mind a tasty trout now and then, either. Beavers, whose palates lean toward poplar and other chewy wood and grass suppers, don't eat trout, as a rule, but their exemplary dam-building clogs high-quality trout streams until their bottoms are shallow and hidden by suspended particles of clay or muck. The slow-moving pools which beavers construct might provide good overhead cover for a trout season or two, but that is about all an angler can or should relate about the lifestyles of flap-tailed and buck-toothed creatures. The dams touted by the beaver's admirers, with their packed and inter-woven stick, mud and weed are minor marvels of design, yes. But instead of serving as lunker-bunkers, the barriers built by most beavers in most places tend to depopulate themselves of trout and other fish in very short order. Were it up to me, beaver colonies in typical trout-supporting watersheds would be broken up on a routine basis, and that no-quarters standard would be applied ruthlessly to publicly-owned lands.

Let's take a close look at some of the trout streams of Allegany State Park, which is the largest single tract of public land within New York, aside from the Adirondack preserve. I hope you and I, with the able assistance of DEC experts, will be able to learn more about this charming fishery—and some of the threats it faces—by referring to authoritative state reports on the subject. Because most of the waters in the park have relatively low trout population densities, this chapter will not spend an inordinate number of pages comparing one stream to another. Instead, it will focus mainly on the precious value of the total resource, and what fisheries experts and anglers alike can do to preserve the park's watery wonders.

By the way, although the author has eaten a few trout in his lifetime, and looks forward to consuming a few more western New York specimens, no wild brookies were killed to facilitate the preparation of this guide book.

Now that I've declared my pedigree—one with which most anglers who fish Allegany State Park feel quite comfortable—I'm going to discuss stocked waters first, then point interested readers toward a dozen or so of the park's better-known and higher-quality streams. It's the only fair way, in my opinion, to compare small, wilderness-type brook trout creeks without causing needless harm to native brookies and wild brown trout which, due to ease of access and heavy angling pressure, have a riskier existence than those faced by their state-park relatives.

We can tackle the hatchery-supplied waters first because, as of this writing, only five streams in the park are on the Department of Environmental Conservation's stocking list. These waters include **Red House Brook, an unnamed tributary of Red House Brook** (called "T-17" by biologists), **Quaker Run**, **Rice Brook**, and **Bay State Brook**. Of the five, Quaker Run is the most heavily stocked and the most popular among regional anglers, as well. Are all those boot tracks along Quaker Run due to the large number of trout in it, or is its stocking quota so big in order to meet the popular demand for those fish? You decide.

Quaker Run strikes me as a good fit, personally, since I caught my first Allegany State Park brookies and browns on its bouncing currents during a long-ago April. They were all eight- and nine-inch fish, lovely to look at, and strong and tenacious when they felt the sting of a hook. The bulk of them were found in little plunge pools and seemed to throw caution to the wind when presented with half-length pieces of night crawlers. Later, I learned that an Adams or a Royal Coachman, both old-time favorite dry-fly patterns, were park-wide trout-takers, but especially in the Run. These and other flashy but suggestive flies appeal to trout everywhere, but I think the reason for their popularity among park-resident fish—brookies and browns alike—is their vague resemblance to all sorts of food items, including beetles and other terrestrial insects as well as floating caddis and mayflies.

The flies just mentioned may not be dead-ringers for any particular bug, but they look good enough for hungry trout to react to their appearance by thinking "yummy." That's the case even during significant mayfly hatches, when it is more important to wade silently and blend into the park's green-and—gray background than to produce an exact imitation of a fluttering dun or egg-toting spinner of any particular species.

Important hatches on Quaker Run and other streams in the southern third of the park, include the Hendricksons, Quill Gordons, Blue Quills, March Browns and even the famous Green Drake. Many of the streams in the park have good numbers of caddis and stone flies, too. Yellow Sallies are common enough to warrant their use from late April into August.

Still, although the appearance of these commonly encountered insects can trigger consistent surface action in the park, its trout are very unlikely to focus on one menu item to the exclusion of all others. Carry a variety of suggestive patterns with you and in most instances they will be more than adequate for the day's fishing.

Averaging about 15- to 20-feet wide in the six-mile stretch between Cain Hollow and Science Lake, Quaker Run is stocked with about 4,000 yearling brown trout and another 200 state-grown two-year-old browns that measure between 12 and 14 inches when they make their first appearances on fish hooks.

One of the more interesting aspects of Quaker Run these days is its prominent role in an ongoing experiment with "Delayed Harvest" trout-fishing regulations. The rules I'm referring to here are designed to give anglers more bang for their license-money bucks. Tried and true for many years in Pennsylvania, the New York concept basically establishes a catch-and-release season in Quaker Run from the first bridge upstream of the Quaker Run (Cain Hollow) upstream to Coon Run Road. In this section, just artificial flies and lures are permitted from April 1 through May 20, and no trout may be creeled until May 21.

The rules spelled out here have a very simple goal, namely, to give sportsmen more water worth fishing in a stretch that was previously thought to be picked clean by late April or mid-May. So far, the Delayed Harvest water in Quaker Run appears to be popular with anglers, at least in part because trout caught three, four or five times in the spring of the year tend to be more aware of their surroundings than any browns fresh from the fish factory. (Take note, please, that current

Delayed Harvest-type rules come from park administration, not from the DEC. Be further advised, if you will, that New York policy currently prohibits stocking any brook trout in the park. If you hook a native here, it's supposed to be the genuine article, born wild.)

When you target Quaker Run, don't neglect to give the wild brookies upstream from Science Lake an hour or two. This part of the stream holds many small brookies, 5 to 7 inches long. It is mostly five to 10 feet wide, and hemmed in by anglers who appreciate the challenge of stalking fish that know how to hide.

Next on the park's hit parade (in the "stocked stream" category) is **Red House Brook**, which used to drop, dip and splash its way north along Allegany State Park Route #2 for a distance of 10 miles. Red House still has a fairly steep gradient, with lots of plunge pools scattered throughout its length, but the brook also has a major habitat problem, thanks to its booming beaver population. Now, I've said it before, yet it still bears repeating, so here we go: "DOWN WITH BEAVERS!" Let us resolve to repeat this simple slogan at every polite opportunity, until it rings in the ears of every fisheries biologist across the fruited plain.

Sportsmen and regional-level Department of Environmental Conservation biologists used to take on beaver population expansions in cooperation with licensed fur trappers and private property owners, and with decent prospects for success. Some years were better than others, of course, for the reason that strong prices in the fur market provided a strong incentive for local experts to go after new colonies throughout the season. In recent years, market prices have been on the low side, at best, and as a result, beavers now seem to pop up just about any place where they aren't wanted. They will continue to make nuisances of themselves until everyone with a stake in the fight stands united against the ruination of trout streams, the flooding of rural roads and other beaver achievements. Among all the fishing holes in Allegany State Park, none has been more devastated in the last couple of decades than Red House Brook.

Why does the state put up with it, you ask me? State government departments such as the Office of Parks, the DEC and even the Department of Transportation are all dependent, in the long run, on constituencies, which basically are groups of supporters, or patrons. As budgets decline and tax rates increase, the patrons who give the most of their time and treasure tend to get the most back in return. Lawmakers aren't stupid; in fact, they are very cagey when the state gets around to carving up and distributing pet projects at the climax of most budget battles.

Any state fisheries biologist who has tried to talk his or her supervisors into giving him a few extra budget bucks or perhaps assigning a couple of muscular summer workers to break up a local beaver dam will attest that the critters have friends in high places. To break up those alliances, let alone win them over, fishermen will have to write lots of letters to legislators, and attend a few public hearings, too. Meanwhile, we can enjoy some fine fishing, even if we have to hike a mile or two to get around the latest mud-and-stick dam.

Red House Brook and its **Tributary-17** are stocked with about 4,400 yearling brown trout, combined, in April. The Red House fish are well-distributed in the system, with about 1,100 yearling browns reserved for planting from Red House Lake downstream for 2 miles to Route 86 (the Southern Tier Expressway). Another 3,300 yearling browns are stocked early in the season from Red House Lake, upstream for 4.8 miles to the mouth of France Brook. Anglers who are in good physical condition can see for themselves what sort of havoc beavers can inflict on trout populations. All they need do is hike in and out of some of the beaver meadows and small dams in the area of the park near France Brook. The damage they'll see is terrific and ongoing. The headwater sections of Red House Brook, including Tributary-17 branches, are far too warm to support stocked fish after later May or early June.

DEC regional fisheries team leader Cornett points out an additional adverse impact of beaver infestation. That is the adoption of dead trees within or close to beaver ponds as ideal nesting, resting, hunting and roosting spots by herons, ospreys and mergansers.

Although it is primarily home, sweet home to stocked trout, Red House Brook has some wild browns, as well. Most of the brownies are in the first 3 miles of the stream's existence, and trout densities aren't heavy enough to warrant intensive angler effort. The stocked fish, however, are hit fairly hard by early-season fishermen. Because it is an average of about 25 feet wide in April and May, Red House Brook is one of the better spots in the park to flex a fly rod. Try that Royal Wulff mentioned a few pages back!

Access to Red House is easy, since it is paralleled by Allegany State Park Route 2 for most of its length.

Two other stocked streams in the park provide fairly good put-and-take trout fishing in April and May. They are **Rice Brook** and **Bay State Brook**.

Rice Brook, which is about eight feet wide in most spots, is on the eastern side of the park and is stocked once annually, in April, with 300 yearling browns. Modest numbers of wild browns and a few wild brook trout share the stream with the stockers. Due to the mix of heavy cover—overgrown fields, first- or second-growth forests and some boggy shrub—fishing pressure is light even in late April, when most other streams in the park are busy. To check it out, readers should take State Park Avenue to the gate on Rice Brook Road.

Bay State Brook is a tributary of lower Red House Brook, and it is seeded with approximately 550 hatchery-reared brown trout April. Ten to 20 years ago, many park visitors rated Bay State as one of the better trout streams in the park, but thanks to numerous beaver dams on the brook and its feeders, the water warms in a hurry after April and May, and old-timers are left to dream of what used to be and might have been. Depending on their experience and skills set, first-time fishers on the eight- to 10-foot-wide streams might report pleasant experiences or conclude that somebody has played a trick on them.

Incidentally, park police stopped charging for an in-park fishing license many years ago, and officials at the police headquarters office are happy to give stream directions to visitors and campers. Free maps and brochures which help rookie fishermen plan their in-park excursions are available, too. It should not come as a surprise that Allegany State Park police, like conservation officers in other regions of New York state, are often good sources of tips pertaining to recent trout fishing.

Although the sight of stocking trucks rolling down the road causes many anglers to feel mildly excited or downright giddy, hatchery-raised transplants are going to play second fiddle to wild brookies; our beloved "natives" whose beauty and struggle to survive makes them unique in the minds of many sportsmen. And it just so happens that natives currently are holding their own in suitable park habitats.

WILD TROUT WATERS OF ALLEGANY PARK

What makes little brookies a big deal to so many trout-fishing fanatics? The passion felt by most of us char-chasers begins with an understanding that natives are on a narrow path between good health and brutal extirpation. The life of a wild brook trout, in most places where the species is found, is lonely and precarious. As our DEC friend Scott Cornett once put it, "nobody who fishes these creeks can expect to run into other anglers and still hope to catch many of the spooky, wild trout that live there." Nor, he might have added, can a conscientious sportsman justify the reaping of a harvest of pink-fleshed, succulent natives in many brook trout waters. Even one or two "keepers" slipped into a wicker creel during a long season might be more losses than some streams can bear. Such considerations are especially important when the fisherman is focused on waters open for public fishing, and Cornett, when asked, usually recommends that anglers show their appreciation for natives by using barbless hooks whether their method of capture is a tiny dry fly, a whirling Mepps spinner or a carton of red worms purchased at a grocery store on the way to a Allegany State Park campground.

Some of the most enchanting places to catch and, hopefully, release, a few natives are in park streams that are managed as wild trout fisheries. Following is a list of ten brooks and creeks, all of which always seem worth fishing, but I'd hesitate to lay them out as a "Top 10." My reluctance is rooted in the strong possibility that one or two streams that have fished very well in recent seasons may drop out of the rankings due to flooding, drought or other adverse circumstances. At the opposite end of the spectrum, it is just as likely that a couple of fishy little rills might improve dramatically in a year or two, as the result of bountiful rainfall or a washout of nearby beaver ponds. It is important for anglers to be aware that what seems like a calamity to them is little more than a nuisance as far as the fish are concerned.

Let's begin our list of hotspots for wild trout in Allegany State Park by exposing a wet finger to the wind and then offering kudos for **Beehunter Creek**, a stream that is comfortably fished by anglers who wear hiking shoes or sneakers instead of hip waders. This nomination may come as a shock to anglers in New York and elsewhere who seldom

In the summer heat, state park fishermen focus their attention on the big shadows cast over the water in mid-day.

STREAMS OF ALLEGANY STATE PARK   67

venture more than a few hundred feet from a public fishing area. One cannot learn much from extended walks along trails and streambanks unless he has also made a habit of reading the "sign" left behind by people at road pull-offs. Foot prints, Styrofoam coffee cups and even torn-off lure packets are unfortunately common these days, wherever an angler goes, but the bare paths which lead away from your car and into a thicket of multi-flora rose usually come to an abrupt ending, and not too far from the highway. My father often opined that folks who have the stamina or stubbornness to go a little farther up or down a thickly covered creek are "real fishermen." He was a marvelous small-stream fisherman, himself, although he was content to fish close to his Syracuse-area home and never set eyes on the Allegany Park. (By the way, the park and the county are spelled that way, i.e., "Allegany," but the mighty river is "Allegheny." I haven't a clue as to why.)

The best fishing in Beehunter Creek begins about half a mile upstream from the cabin area and continues another mile and a half to the very headwaters. It's a hike-in stream, with access limited to those who can lay down their own light prints as they go. Wild brookies, rarely longer than 8 inches but plentiful in smaller sizes, are the rewards at journey's end. Surprisingly, in-stream sampling of Beehunter in 2008 resulted in an estimate that the creek's entire population of brook trout included no more than 169 adults! Surely it has more natives than that by this time.

McIntosh Creek is another fine park stream that has the distinction of being targeted for stream-improvement work under the auspices of Trout Unlimited. That is an enduring compliment, even if the job is still a work in progress. TU is an international conservation organization whose membership roster has occasionally included me and some of my friends, too. The group always has good intentions and sometimes has spectacular success with its trout stream makeovers, which are usually carried out with the cooperation of the Army Corps of Engineers or the U.S. Fish and Wildlife Service. Having rolled a few rocks and diagrammed a couple of wing dams, myself, I can appreciate the fact that some projects pan out and some do not. At this writing, the jury is still out on the McIntosh Creek undertaking, but we all have our fingers crossed.

McIntosh Creek is a two-mile-long tributary of Red House Lake. It can be accessed from the lower end of Allegany State Park Route 1 or by walking upstream from the cabin-camping area. In 2008, hard-working volunteers laid out tools and then rolled up their sleeves and got to work at 17 sites along the creek. Their plan was to create or enhance pools that would boost the stream's adult trout population and, hopefully, make it more hospitable to larger brook trout such as the eight- and nine-inchers which had contributed to McIntosh Creek's glowing reputation among western New York anglers.

But when project organizers conducted follow-up visits to evaluate the stream's trout population from 2009 through 2012 they re-learned some ancient truths. First, it's hard work for a few adults to build trout pools by moving some rocks around. On the other hand, it is relatively easy for floods—which are common in Allegany Park—to undo some of the good deeds offered up by earnest volunteers. Besides, what Ma Nature overlooks might seem like fair game to campground kids who are just looking for something to build or un-build on a hot summer's afternoon.

When the McIntosh data were analyzed, project leaders found that the 17 tree and wood pool structures were occupied by brookies, but did not result in any significant increases in the total trout population. Researchers did find large year-to-year swings in the numbers of adult brookies in both Beehunter and McIntosh creeks. They also confirmed that floods often account for the loss of hundreds of young-of-year natives in tiny mountain brooks.

While waiting for good things to happen to favorite fishing holes in the state park, brook trout anglers can fill empty hours by prospecting in unfamiliar waters. One that's well worth exploring is **Stoddard Creek**, which, like Beehunter and McIntosh creeks, is a tributary of Red House Lake. Wild brookies are the main attraction in Stoddard, but it also has a reputation for giving some wild browns a good place to live. Either a 10-inch brown or an eight-inch native would be worthy of a whistle, or perhaps a close-up photo.

Scott Cornett advises anglers to focus on Stoddard Creek from the Red House campground for about 2 miles. Below this stretch, habitat is mediocre, at best. The creek is not as hard to walk as some others in the park, since it is closely shadowed by Allegany State Park Route 1.

Next on the park hit list are a couple of feeders of Quaker Run, namely, **English Creek** and **Coon Run**. Many anglers rate English Creek as the best tributary of Quaker Run but Coon Run can't be far behind. A major plus for both streams is their healthy populations of both brown and brook trout. One thing that might set English Creek apart from other park waters is its close proximity to park Route 1. As for Coon Run, it is best approached by fishermen who are willing to hike upstream for a mile or so along Coon Run Road. A locked gate at the end of this trek reminds anglers that they are about to walk into the state of Pennsylvania.

A third Quaker Run tributary is **Stony Brook**, which has essentially been ruined by a network of beaver dams. This stream looks very tempting in its lower reaches, but is too warm to support a large trout population. Fishermen who check it out will find a wild brown or brookie here or there, but not in any numbers.

The lower segment of **Rice Brook**, as mentioned earlier, is stocked annually with brown trout and fishes reasonably well in the early weeks of the trout season. Many anglers, however, will prefer the water upstream from where Irish Brook merges into Rice Brook. Above Irish Brook, it is approximately 3 miles to Rice Brook's headwaters, and the entire stream holds a mix of browns and brookies. Beavers are annoying here, but not yet as destructive as they are in some other park neighborhoods.

Limestone Brook certainly merits a mention wherever Allegany State Park fishing prospects are being discussed. Located on the east side of the park, Limestone twists and turns from start to finish, and the undercuts and little plunge pools that result hold both brookies and browns. The lower mile and a half of the brook shines even though much of it cuts across private land and even back yards. If you had an afternoon to fish and wanted to cap your outing by hooking a foot-long trout, you could do worse than to focus on this stretch. A hard strike on a wet fly or a small Panther Martin spinner might break the foot-long barrier in the first mile or so upstream from the park boundary, too. Limestone Brook Road runs alongside the stream, and it can be worth your while to drop a garden worm or a salted minnow into any tributary that intrigues you, especially if the feeder creek flows through a shadowy culvert pool.

If you are looking for a couple of park streams that are under-fished, consider **Wolf Run**. In fact, you might try it in the month of May, when New York's spring turkey season is in full swing. The southwest sector of the state park, through which Wolf Run meanders, is infested by beavers and also happens to be bordered by the state of Pennsylvania as well as the Seneca Nation of Indians' reservation. Before you plan a trout and turkey "cast and blast" in this area of the park, have a chat with a knowledgeable officer of the Park Police about where New York begins and the other places end. With good directions, and perhaps a couple of owl hoots or crow calls along the Wolf Road, you should be able to pick a good spot to hunt within 500 to 750 yards of your parked car.

Remember, New Yorkers have to "call it a day" by noon. Personally, instead of driving back to the park campground or motel you might be staying at and then changing into trout gear, I would simply lock my shotgun or bow in my vehicle, and immediately carry my rod and creel into the thick cover along Wolf Run. Doing it that way will save you a good 45 minutes. Be forewarned, however, that the trek into the better parts of the stream and the return trip to your parked car can be a little treacherous, especially when the sun is slipping beneath the steep hills in the southwest sector of the park.

To assure a safe walk in or out of this fairly rugged park, wear a Blaze Orange cap and put a 12 × 12-inch square of hot orange on your back, too.

The park is bisected by dozens of un-stocked but trout-friendly brooks, some of which could fill out a "top 10" ranking. Among the worthies are **Bova Creek**, in the Red House Lake watershed, which holds both browns and natives; and **Fox Hollow**, which is part of the Quaker Run system and holds brookies, only. If push came to shove, I'd settle for a top 10 that leaves Stony Brook to the beavers instead of fishermen.

I hope you noticed that I neglected to do a formal rating of the state park's streams. Sometimes, statistics don't tell the whole story. It would be nice to let the angler who slips and slides his way upstream after the next summer gully-washer to devise his own scoring system for park trout. Coming back just in time for supper, with a tired grin on his face, will be reward enough for him.

CHAPTER FOUR

Allegany County

GENESEE RIVER

RATING: ★★★★★ (5 stars)
BEST TIME: The last week of May through the first week of June.
BEST METHOD: Stalk individual trout rising to feed on hatching mayflies.

My first impression of the upper Genesee River, which crosses the Pennsylvania-New York border near Shongo and from there flows north through Wellsville, Belmont and the Letchworth canyon on its way to meet with Lake Ontario at Rochester, was everything I expected. For three nights in a row, retired Syracuse firefighter Mike Brilbeck and I ate cold pizza, convenience-shop sandwiches and other very late suppers of dubious dining distinction, just to make sure we did not miss out on the river's fast and furious hatch-matching. With sulfur-colored mayflies swarming all around me, I caught four brown trout between 20 and 22 inches long, as well as a dozen or so smaller fish. Despite warmer than normal air and water temperatures, the trout lined up just below the surface. From 7 p.m. until after dark, they fed ravenously, as if they were partaking of their last meal, ever. With intense concentration, Brilbeck and I could almost pre-measure the trout we stalked, by noting the spaces between each fish's dorsal and caudal fins. Toward the end of these spectacles, we were as picky as the fish, and focused solely

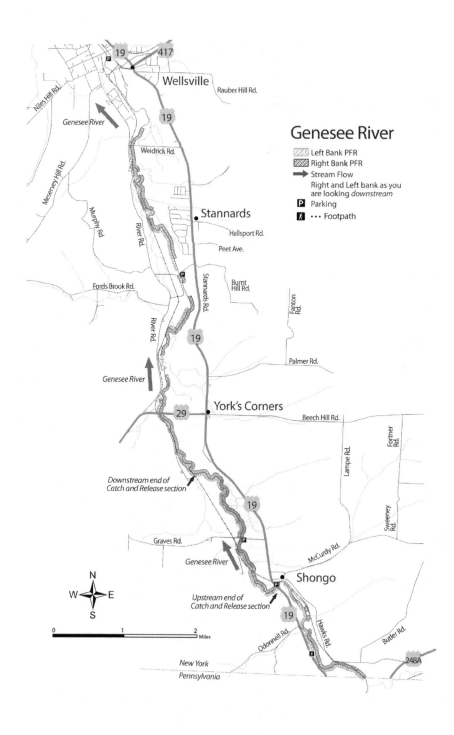

Genesee River

- ▨ Left Bank PFR
- ▨ Right Bank PFR
- ➤ Stream Flow
  Right and Left bank as you
  are looking *downstream*
- 🅿 Parking
- 🚶 ⋯ Footpath

19 417

Wellsville

Niles Hill Rd.

Rauber Hill Rd.

19

Genesee River

Weidrick Rd.

Meserve Hill Rd.

Murphy Rd.

River Rd.

Stannards

Hallsport Rd.

Peet Ave.

Ford Brook Rd.

Stannards Rd.

Burnt
Hill Rd.

Fanton
Rd.

19

Palmer Rd.

River Rd.

Genesee River

York's Corners

29

Beech Hill Rd.

Fortner
Rd.

Lampe Rd.

Downstream end of
Catch and Release section

19

Sweeney
Rd.

Graves Rd.

Genesee River

McCurdy Rd.

Shongo

Upstream end of
Catch and Release section

19

N
W   E
S

0   1   2 Miles

Odonnell Rd.

Hawks Rd.

Butler Rd.

248A

New York
Pennsylvania

on those which daintily poked their snouts through the surface and left only the quietest ripples on the water. Most such trout, we knew, were sizable specimens that would slip into the shadows to capture and consume spent egg-layers as they drifted downstream along the current edges. Any mayfly that put up the slightest fight against its impending demise, with its abdomen trembling and tattered wings bent every which way, was assumed to be an emerging nymph, but if we had any doubt whether we were confronted by emergers or spinners, we bent low over the water to intercept a few "unknowns" with aquarium nets. As the sun disappeared behind the ancient, flat-topped mountains of Allegany County, the insects still on the water wriggled desperately. A lucky few might get away before a hungry trout dragged them into oblivion.

The hatches were heavy that trip, which spanned the first week of June, but the best part of the trip was the almost total absence of other fishermen. Now and then during our five-day visit, one or two anglers would turn into the parking area adjacent to the Route 19 bridge at Shongo, but nobody joined us at the bridge pool or the long flat just

The large pool crossed by Route 19 south of Wellsville offers great access to the no-kill area on the Genesee River.

downstream for the reliable spinner flight at dark. Their loss, I suppose! Anyway, I have never encountered much competition on this river, which is one of New York's best and possibly the top trout stream in the western region of the state.

As to Allegany County on the whole, it has at least a dozen healthy trout streams of fishable size flowing through its farms and small towns, but the Genny between the Pennsylvania border and the towns of Wellsville and Belmont deserves recognition as the best in the region, and its supporters could make a strong case that this challenging river is one of the top five or 10 in the Empire State. Of course, the presence of a 2½-mile-long catch-and-release fishing area, (known locally as simply "the No-Kill") doesn't do any harm to the stream's reputation. Thanks to the constant string of "put backs"—my term for the safe and sound releases which DEC biologists and conservation officers require of fishermen who enjoy the Shongo catch-and-release water—sportsmen can rest assured that many sizable brown and rainbow trout are available for the catching from late March or early April until late June or so, when warming air and water forces the mostly hatchery-bred residents of the No-Kill to look upriver and down for pools that are well shaded, spring-cooled and still pleasant to fish. Later, in the autumn months, the DEC boosts the Genesee's reputation by dropping off a tanker truckload of hatchery brood stock in the No-Kill. Some of these are five- to 10-pound beauties. The fish come from the Randolph hatchery or the Bath hatchery, in Steuben County—and sometimes both facilities have a few left-overs for this popular program.

When I first heard about the breeder-release program back in the late 1990s, I asked one of my DEC contacts if the participating fish liked their "retirement plan." He replied that he wasn't sure, because he had never actually discussed it with the trout. However, he added, many anglers had broached the subject with him over the years, and not a single one had ever described himself as a dissatisfied customer.

Any outdoors writer who has shaken hands or told a joke or accepted a beer during a local rod and gun club's monthly meeting or Christmas party would be surprised, indeed, to meet a state worker who didn't keep one nervous eye on the door when he was the "guest of honor" at a club function. Few serious debates with regard to license fees, gun-control regulations or other hot-button topics are resolved over a single game dinner, no matter how good the food tastes. Most of the time, repeated phone calls, emails and other exchanges are part of the process, and the end result is a compromise that individual sportsmen may or may not find to their liking. That's the way it works, and if you don't believe me, ask your DEC regional fisheries manager, who has to take considerable flak every two years when he and his superiors in Albany put dozens of proposed regulatory changes up for public review.

Yet the vast majority of anglers who live in western New York fully support the state hatchery workers and fisheries biologists who give those big rainbows and browns a place to hang out in their twilight years. By that time, the "retirees" no longer need much of anything, but a good number of them will keep on hammering big streamer flies and tight-wobbling stick baits and probably scaring the wits out of unsuspecting fishermen between Shongo and Belmont, too. The upper Genny is perfect for this annual mission because it is big enough to hide two-feet-long trout, and can also accommodate plenty of anglers.

This 21-inch brown trout which the author hooked on a sulfur dry about 1,000 yards below the Shongo bridge over Route 19 was released in good condition after all the fun.

The breeders are set free in the fall, when the river generally runs low but cold, and fishing pressure is virtually non-existent. Oh, a few diehards will make a last-chance, overnight trip to Genesee country, but if their experiences are like mine, they stand an excellent chance of hooking a hatchery survivor—or nothing at all. To give readers an idea of the difficult fishing that the Genny serves up to its fans during the autumn months, consider another trip Brilbeck and I took four years ago. The fish were rising faster than the Pillsbury Dough Boy when we arrived, and there must have been 50 or more brown and rainbow trout holding near the surface in the shadows beneath the Route 19 bridge.

We gave it our best shot, but how many trout could we hope to catch when all within our casting range were taking bugs so tiny we could not quite identify their genus and species under a magnifying glass? The few I managed to dip-net from the water's surface were not mayflies, but might have been midges or even emerging midge larvae. I suppose I should have taken a few specimens home for a closer look, but I haven't worried much about such procedures lately. It's probably a middle-age thing. Anyway, the little wigglies were smaller than the hook size number 24 Little Olives and Trico duns and spinners I kept in a hidden fly-vest pocket—just in case I ever had to use such a minuscule fly.

The whopper breeders which supposedly cause many anglers to return to the Genesee valley each year were nowhere to be found during that trip, but I was back again the following April, in the forlorn hope that heavy mayfly action would get the season off to a solid start.

Many anglers who travel widely from the Catskills to the Adirondacks in search of rising trout and even save a little vacation time for waters in central and western New York think they're hearing things when a fellow fan of cold water fisheries points them to the upper Genny.

"Oh, you mean the one that's in Rochester," says somebody who has done the Pacific salmon and steelhead runs in that city.

And I reply that, no, in context he must be thinking of the same Genesee but the part of it at the other end. The Genny I have in mind is just a couple of miles north of the New York-Pennsylvania border. By now, I might be rolling my eyes in exasperation, for I've had this discussion over and over, with fly fishermen whose wanderlusts have taken them fishing all over the country—yet they can't find the better parts of the Genesee River on an old-fashioned map. The simplest way to resolve the issue is to grab a good old DeLorme *Atlas* and poke the river I'm thinking of with my pointed index finger. Maybe, if I'm in a sharing mood, I might elaborate a little, showing where the Genny crosses the border and flows through Shongo, the town (Belmont) where a warming seasonal sun replaces trout with smallmouth bass and, approximately 80 miles north on the map, the spot where smallmouth bass, walleyes and other warm- or cool-water critters swim downstream and rush through crowds of steelhead fisherman and into Lake Ontario.

Coming from the Syracuse area, my fishing friends and I generally take the Thruway west to the Geneva exit, then go right onto U.S. Route 20 and, after driving west for a couple of miles, turn left onto Route 245. We take that road southwest to the village of Naples, in Ontario County. Next, I'd recommend consulting with whoever serves as your trip navigator—a role that Tom-Tom or a real, live person can play, and then taking Route 21 south from Naples to North Cohocton, Wayland, and North Hornell. Keep rolling west on Route 21 south to Andover, then hang a right onto Route 417. From this intersection, you have only about a 10-minute drive to Wellsville. Dyke Creek, a very fishy-looking tributary, runs along on your right virtually the entire way.

Once you're in Wellsville, you can check in at your motel, and, if you wish, immediately head south on Route 19. There are plenty of enticing pools along the way, but my personal preference is to keep going until I get to Shongo, where the state line is only about 1.5 miles shy of the Pennsylvania border via Hawks Road or Route 19. Much more important, for getting-around purposes, the bridge at Shongo marks the starting point of one of the state's more productive special-regulations areas. The aforementioned 2.5-mile catch-and-release section is very good fishing down to Wellsville, and visiting anglers within that stretch or, for that matter, above or below the No-Kill. Using a DEC map of the Genny which can be downloaded from the agency's web site, www. dec.ny.gov, anybody who can feel his way along a computer keyboard will be able to find logical entry points for fishermen at several spots down-river, starting with the Graves Road crossing, York's Corners, Jack Bridge, the village of Stannards and several street crossings within the Wellsville town limits. That last suggestion refers primarily to flood-control channels that are stocked heavily and therefore are visited regularly by local bait fishermen and spinning enthusiasts.

During the annual Greater Wellsville Trout Derby, which is held the last weekend of April, hundreds of anglers fish for browns and rainbows which are pre-fitted with numbered tags that are good for cash prizes. Some of the largest trout entered in the derby are yanked out of some of the large pools and deep runs in good old downtown Wellsville. Watch your step if you plan on getting close to the water by taking hops, skips and jumps along the sloping rip-rap that holds the river bank in place. Few if any of the cash awards handed out during the contest will pay for fixing your broken leg!

One more stretch of the upper Genny that merits a thorough try in April and May, at the very least, is the junction of Knights Creek and the Genesee, about 20 miles north of the Pennsylvania border.

Oak Duke, a fellow writer-editor who has the good fortune to live and work almost literally within casting range of the Genny, told me once that anyone who finds the big river too crowded, too muddy or too anything when they're trying for trout makes a huge mistake by heading home early. When Oak is frustrated by the Genny's trout, he checks the water temperature. If readings have crept into the low 70s, he temporarily adjusts his mindset from "big brown" to "big bass." When rising temperatures cause big brownies to feel a little lethargic, river bass often come to life.

When the switch-over takes place, smallmouths go for live crayfish, shiner minnows, and lots of other big baits. In-line spinners, such as C.P. Swings and almost any Mepps spinner will produce, as well. But even more action is heading the angler's way, if he happens to be a skilled fly caster. Knot a black or olive Wooly Bugger streamer, a mouse imitation fashioned from roughly trimmed deer hair, or a Clouser Minnow with dumbbell eyes to your leader. A 10-pound tippet is recommended, especially if you are planning to do a fair amount of roll casting.

If it takes you a few hours to get a grip on smallmouth techniques, remind yourself that these are not just any old smallmouths. Genesee smallmouths, which share pools with stocked and holdover trout, commonly measure 14 to 16 inches, and three- or four-pounders are there for the catching. Just don't expect them to be easy to hook, for the wariness and keen vision of sight-feeding river smallmouths are worthy of any trout angler's admiration. When the going gets tough, focus on making quiet, drag-free presentations, whether you are likely to be using fly, lure or bait.

Are any of you hatch-matching, fly-flinging fanatics ready to throw in your crying towels?

I wouldn't think of saying farewell to other Genesee River fans without giving them a few fly patterns and tactics for future use.

First, this river has fair to very good hatches, more days than not, beginning shortly after the season opens on April Fool's Day and continuing into early October. Sure, there some lulls along the way, but not many. The main problem with the Genny, in terms of trip-planning, is not any lack of aquatic insects, but an overabundance of warm water. Its meandering path through a wide river valley guarantees the Genny will always be a challenge to fish during the summer months. At the same time, though, the succession of hatches that I have looked forward to in recent years include a couple of very good trout-takers for the early season, April 1–15. This time frame takes in some impressive, sunny-afternoon bursts of surface activity that are composed mainly of tiny Blue Quills, tied on light-wire size 20 dry-fly hooks; along with size 12 or 14 Quill Gordons, and the Genesee's prolific assortment of size 14–20 little Blue-Winged Olives. With the addition of a dozen or more Hendrickson dries and/or emergers wrapped onto size 14 and 16 hooks, you should be reasonably well equipped for any early-season trout encounters.

I've learned to appreciate the Dark Haystack and Light Haystack fashioned by the late Francis Betters for use on the Adirondacks' churning West Branch of the Ausable River. In his small tackle shop on Route 86, which was a short walk downstream from the legendary Flume Pool, Betters would whip up dozens of Haystacks, and then urge customers to make certain they had enough of the day's hottest flies, just in case. The Haystacks—which work especially well in pocket water, and continue to sell like the proverbial hot cakes—are still tied and promoted by their true believers throughout the Northeastern United States. If you don't tie, yourself, you should at least have no difficulty finding a few reasonable imitations in local tackle shops.

Tying flies is easy. Don't worry much about the color of a "dark" or "light" Haystack, because your goal is to come up with two or three hues that will work on your rivers, and not merely the next time you motor upstate to the Adirondacks. Here's the pattern:

1. Wind white or orange thread and load it on a bobbin in your usual manner. Cover the hook shank (any dry fly hook between sizes 10 and 20 is okay) with the thread and wind it back to a point just ahead of the bend.

2. Wax the thread, about 2 inches at a time, and use it to tie a clump of deer hair, about 8 or 10 hairs in all, just ahead of the hook bend. Pinch down firmly but not enough to snap the thread. This pinch of hair should be about as long as the hook shank.

3. After tying the "tail" of deer hair in place, wind the thread forward and prepare a second clump of deer hair to be used as an upright wing. Tie it down on the hook, firmly (not too much so, however) and relax it ever so slowly and for only a few seconds. The wing should splay atop the hook shank, so that the deer hair tips are shaped like a fluttering mayfly wing.

4. Now wind the thread back and forth, behind and in front of the splayed wing. Tie a couple of half hitches to the rear of the wing, then use a couple of drops of clear nail polish to make sure it holds in place.

5. Finally, select a pinch of your favorite fur dubbing material, natural or synthetic, and daub it to the dangling thread. Wind it back to where the tail is affixed to the hook, then back again to a point just in front of the deer-hair wing. Do it a tiny bit at a time, so as to cover the thread completely without making the fly look too bulky.

I was supposed to tell you a color combination, right? Well, there's no need to be too mysterious. Simply pick a dark clump of deer hair, and choose a body material which looks to be slightly more brown than the buck or doe that gave itself up for your cause. Do it the same way as you match a light cream-hued clump of deer hair for your "Light Haystack." Mission accomplished!

The Haystack Fly

The most obvious attribute of a Haystack is its consistent floatability. Fishermen also love their versatility. With a little imagination, an angler can float a Haystack downstream, dead-drift, to trout that are feeding on mayfly spinners. Or, he could easily swing the 'stack down and across, so that it resembles a caddis or evening a mayfly dun that is trying to lay its eggs on or near the river's surface.

As surely as April is followed by May, the hatches coming off the water on this day or that will include a blizzard of bugs that are, for the most part, bigger and lighter in color than those you expected in the first six or eight weeks of the season. One of Betters' reliable old Haystacks will fill in nicely until perfection comes floating down the Genesee's surface. Those readers who worry that the Haystack is too much of the same-old, same-old to fool modern trout can take the evolution of fly patterns to the next step, as angling authors Al Caucci and Bob Nastasi did when they published *Hatches* in 1975. They modified Betters' Haystack approach by leaving the deer hair wings intact but replacing the deer hair tails with more realistic hackle barbs or fine paint brush bristles. Kudos to them, and to Fran Betters' legacy, as well.

The Genesee River isn't pounded by as many wading boots as the more famous rivers in the Catskills, but it is a great teacher for anglers in thirst of knowledge. In fact, it is probably as fine a classroom for anglers as any other I've found. Region 9 Fisheries biologists and technicians confirmed my glowing assessment of this Southern Tier jewel in 2010, when they implemented a Genesee River angler diary program. Only 13 of the 50 fishermen who signed up for the project actually turned in their completed data books at the end of the study period (March-October), but the information they jotted down after each and every fishing trip in the river was most helpful to fisheries managers. The baker's dozen of participants reported going on 209 trips and logging 702 angler-hours on the Genny in 2010. During the project, 79 percent of all the effort expended by diary-keepers was completed in April, May and June. They logged the capture of 499 yearling brown trout, of which 96 percent were released. Another 213 two-year-old or older brownies were landed, and 91 percent of those trout were caught and released.

Are you starting to get the idea that a strong catch-and-release ethic has taken hold of Genesee River anglers? Then you should be proud to know that the survey by diaries showed that all 14 brook trout caught

Sean Kelly waits for Hendrickson mayfly hatch to commence on the upper "Jenny."

in the study area, and 98 percent of the 178 rainbows reported in the diaries were turned loose by their captors. The cumulative catch rate of trout by anglers taking part in the study was 1.33 browns and/or rainbows per hour. That's well above the management objective for most trout streams in New York, which is one trout per two hours.

Studies like the one conducted in 2010 and repeated in 2014 with similar results, tell us that the Genesee is a boon for research and recreation, alike. Newcomers who wonder what the Genny might have to offer in a typical year can reasonably expect to find decent hatches and rising trout on the river almost any time from April 15 through the end of June. While summer fishing always slows down as cold-blooded trout are forced by warming temperatures to search for a cooler hang-out, even that dire situation can be rectified by a few timely downpours in July or August. When and if the water rises, it is surprising how many temperature refugees can show up, almost overnight, to make a hearty meal of hatching mayflies, caddis or terrestrial insects which tumble into the river from overhanging trees.

It is no wonder, then, why the Genesee's loyalists toss and turn in their beds at night, dreaming of mid-season thunderstorms that are capable of bringing flash-flooding to a small watershed in a couple of hours.

The Genesee River is stocked yearly with 20,600 yearling brown trout and 2,300 two-year-old browns. It also gets about 6,200 yearling rainbows from the Randolph hatchery. As a bonus, the DEC usually has a number of breeders—dozens or hundreds—available from Randolph. They are stocked in the autumn months when their services are deemed to be no longer needed, and anglers who prowl the No-Kill or, for that matter, any of the deep pools between the Shongo bridge and Belmont, have a gambler's chance of tying into a monster before the firearms season for deer begins. Few trout anglers are still on the water after that.

About 18 miles of public fishing rights are available along the Genesee, which, if not truly crowded by anglers, has a longstanding reputation as one of the most heavily fished streams in New York. It is also one of those rivers that can be tamed, in places, by anglers with physical challenges. Accessible casting platforms at Island Park in Wellsville and at the Route 19 bridge over the Belmont dam can be fished from a wheelchair.

Although the Genesee is the local "Queen of Waters"—and that wet fly happens to be a good one to drift and swing along the river's edge—her court consists of several other tributaries that are worth prospecting any time of the year. Several of these small streams hitch their currents to those of the Genny in or near downtown Wellsville, and a few others slink and meander through the more rural neighborhoods in Allegany County. More than a couple of streams in this part of the state have even been known to dive underground now and then in search of colder temperatures.

DYKE CREEK

RATING: ★★★ (3 stars)

BEST TIME TO FISH: Late April, when the creek's water warms daily into the high 50s or even the low 60s. That's pretty close to perfect for browns, whether stocked or held-over from the previous year.

BEST METHODS: Bottom-bounce using a multiple-fly rig. Hang a weighted stonefly nymph on the tippet and one or two wet flies of your choice attached with 3- or 4-inch droppers, spread 12 to 18 inches apart. Alternately, go up and across with a Panther Martin spinner and retrieve at a fast pace.

It may not be your idea of a great-looking trout stream. Heck, I was a little put off, myself, when I first explored Dyke Creek. The 15-foot-wide creek that bubbles and bends from its spring-fed beginnings just upstream (east) of the village of Andover and then flows westward to meet the Genesee in Wellsville is a good example of the price people used to pay for flood control. These days, highway departments and military engineers know that straightening stream channels and using dikes to contain them is akin to moving your water woes downstream. Instead of doing things the old-fashioned way, modern flood-fighters try to slow runaway streams down by constructing meanders or even small side channels.

Dyke Creek, sorry to say, got the old-style flood cure, as one can tell by looking at the 20- or 30-foot tall dikes which run parallel to Route 417. This channelizing must have been devastating for trout habitat, at first. In the last several years, however, my fishing companions and I have opted to ignore the creek's plain looks and focus, instead, on its very fishable water. The choppy riffles and runs and the occasional deep pools all seem to hold a nice fish or two. One morning in April, 2016, when my son Sean and I were frustrated by the frigid water temperatures in the Genesee River, we opted to try spinning lures and garden worms behind a closed industrial plaza adjacent to Route 417, just outside the Wellsville village limits. Each of us was rewarded by hard strikes and fierce tug-o-wars with 15-inch brown trout. They weren't racing each other to get to our offerings, but the sleek and colorful fish we landed were suitable repayment for the diligence we had invested in the trip. In fact, I wondered if my 15-incher might have been stream-bred. DEC caretakers have found modest populations of brown and even brook trout in or near several of Dyke Creek's small tributaries.

Although you might land a wild one on rare occasions, most trout in Dyke Creek are hatchery products, and the stream is managed as a put-and-take fishery. It is stocked with about 2,900 yearling browns and another 200 two-year-olds in April. Skilled fly-fishers can find browns

Sean Kelly fishing on Dyke Creek.

feeding at the surface on caddis adults starting in early May. Most of the insects fluttering at eye level or swooping from brushy limbs on May evenings are imitated by flies with deer hair or elk hair wings—such as the simply named but world-famous Elk Hair Caddis—and have abdomens mimicked by dubbed olive, tan or charcoal gray abdomens.

Because Dyke Creek runs through a wide valley with a shortage of shady cover, much of the stream is marginally suitable for trout habitat by mid-June or so. That does not mean it isn't worth fishing, but if you're traveling a significant distance to try your luck, you can increase your catch by carefully planning your visits. Instead of driving to the stream at mid-day or after a warm spell, be sure to get there before dusk (and sleep over in a local motel), or get up very early on a summer's day, so you will be fishing when temperatures are at their coolest level for this time of the year. That same advice, of course, applies to mid-summer fishing in any stream which has seasonal fluctuation of air and water temperatures.

CHENUNDA CREEK

RATING: ★★★ (3 stars)

BEST TIME TO FISH: If you are inclined to fish for wild trout, and not settle for stocked fish, Chenunda Creek has produced some dandy specimens during DEC electrofishing studies, and one of the best times to catch such fish is on the opening day of the trout season. No April Fooling!

BEST METHOD: For all the needling bait-dunkers put up with over the years, dead-drifting a nightcrawler through deep pools is a great way to catch the 20-inchers that live in this underappreciated stream.

Now, I wouldn't want to get readers unduly excited, but DEC electrofishing teams have indeed captured and physically examined several impressive brown trout during recent population surveys in Chenunda Creek. In 2013, their haul included one brownie that measured just over 22½ inches and change from end to end. Although that was a dandy by anybody's standards, I'm sure most anglers understand that such fish are hard to find and harder to catch. But that's my only disclaimer. The fact that this brown or that was not caught last season makes its capture more likely, not less so, this season. (Maybe we should excuse ourselves and hit the stream banks now instead of later.)

The number one determinant of fishing success, I firmly believe, is the amount of time serious anglers spend on the water with rod in hand. All other factors being equal, the man or woman who spends the most time fishing on high quality, trout-choked rivers, creeks and brooks is going to out-fish the competition, more often than not.

Chenunda Creek links up with the Genesee River in the village of Stannards. It is stocked annually with about 1,300 yearling browns, between Roeske Road and Hallsport. You can find the creek by driving along County Route 248 in the towns of Willing and Independence. It's quite small, for the most part, although it does have a number of deep pools and log jams capable of hiding good-size browns. Woods and partially overgrown pastures which signal abandoned farm land do provide some decent shady cover in the summer months, but the creek has a noticeable suburban feel to it as it slips into Wellsville and heads for the rendezvous with the Genesee. Unless you encounter one of those extreme posted signs—the ones that read something like "No Fishing, No Questions, Violators Will be Shot"—you should be able to get permission to drop a line or two from a few landowners in the neighborhood. In fact, the standard "no trespassing" signs may prove to be your gateway to new fishing spots this year.

As DEC officials have explained about posted lands throughout the state, signs often go up because the landowner desires to know who fishes on his property—period. Others are disinclined to permit hunting on their property, but have no objections to fishing, per se. Littering, foul language and other behavioral issues tend to keep up the keep out signs. So, why not show up with a plastic bag the next time you're calling on a landowner to seek permission to trespass? Fill it as full as you can, and say you'll do it again the next time you fish.

While Chenunda Creek has no public fishing signs along its banks, posting is limited to a few places, and the DEC will likely continue to stock the stream unless there's a sudden eruption of posting in the neighborhood.

LINE COLOR REALLY DOES MATTER
TO SPINNING EXPERTS

Trout fishers who stick mostly to spinning gear and tactics have a reputation for being casual but I'm here to tell you, it's a bum rap. The difference between fact and fiction in this case is that most anglers get into the trout game one hip boot at a time. They simply want to be sure they're going to enjoy trout fishing—and all the big spending that seems to go with it. So, as I see it, they're not casual, they're cautious, and that strikes me as only proper.

I am well-acquainted with several expert spin-fishers, and not one of them can be considered casual about any aspect of trout fishing. They are, in truth, every bit as fussy about the terminal tackle and the lures in their fishing-vest pockets as the snobbiest of dry fly purists can be about their tippet lengths and their ability to reach rising fish under difficult circumstances.

Conducting an informal poll among several fishing buddies regarding spinning tackle, I found solid support for ultralight gear, including rods of 5½ or 6 feet in length, and a small but smooth-running reel that's capable of holding 150 yards of 4-pound-test monofilament.

The most important part of this rig, assuming the reel is func-tioning properly and not curling up into a bird's-nest snarl every other cast, is the line. My pal John "Kid" Corbett, the retired police lieutenant, gives a ringing endorsement to lines that are clear blue in color. The water and sky, more days than not, make it easy enough for an angler to follow the progress of his retrieved lure. At the same time, trout get a poor look, or even no look, at lures retrieved against a sunny backdrop. Or so Kid tells me, and he's got some good photographs to back him up.

In addition to that clear-blue mono, Corbett spoke for many spinning enthusiasts when he offered the following tips:

1. Use a stainless wire snap, not a snap swivel, when you are attaching a plug to your line. The action is better. On the other hand, try a snap swivel with an in-line spinner or a wobbling lure.

2. If water clarity and color give you a chance to watch the lure during your retrieve, don the best pair of sunglasses with polarized lenses that you own.

3. Use your brightest, shiniest lures you own on blue-sky days. However, go for something with a darker finish—possibly one of those ultra-realistic stickbaits—when skies or overcast or even threatening.

4. Spinners will get you the most fish, but the bigger trout will be more likely to strike on Rapala-type stickbaits.

CRYDER CREEK

RATING: ★★★ (3 stars)

BEST TIME TO FISH: When the stocking trucks have made their last run of the season, probably in late April.

BEST METHOD: Old-style worm-dunking, replete with forked sticks for rod-watching.

The last time my son and I tried our luck in Western New York, we followed a rural road down a short hill and crossed Cryder Creek. One car was parked by the bridge, and yellow and green signs courtesy of the DEC confirmed my initial impression that this stream would almost certainly be angler-friendly. One fisherman was stationed on the upstream side of the crossing; the rest was open to Sean or me, as we chose. Heeding my suggestion to try worms, Sean clambered down a steep bank and began fishing.

I inquired about the other fellow's action or lack thereof and was pleased to hear him respond that he needed only one more fish for his limit. He was using a spinner of some sort and had one 11-inch

Sean Kelly fishes the somewhat remote Cryder Creek, known for its nice brown trout.

brown plus three in the 9- or 10-inch range. Wishing him well, I did a wide circle around his spot and found another nice pool a bit farther upstream. After an absence of half an hour or so, I returned to find that the other gentleman had caught number five, while Sean had landed and released a nice one, maybe 13 or even 14 inches long, and was working on another. I wound up hooking and losing a foot-long brown but that was it for me.

A little follow-up investigation of Cryder Creek yielded some useful information. First, I learned that this stream has a loyal following among sportsmen in southern Allegany County and also a fair number of fishermen who hail from northern Potter County, Pennsylvania. The creek first shows up, in my DeLorme's *Atlas & Gazetteer*, east of Shongo. It slides into the Genesee River just south of the Pennsylvania/ New York border. First, find Shongo on your map, and use your soft Number 2 pencil or a pinkie finger to follow Route 19 south a couple of miles across the border, then turn left onto Route 248A.

Route 248A heads upstream (northeast) along Cryder Creek, for about 10 miles, to the community of Whitesville. Go a bit farther on

248A or Route 6 and you will cross the line between Allegany County and Steuben County. Upstream from here, the stream you're looking at is officially called Marsh Creek.

The DEC stocks Cryder Creek annually with around 2,600 yearling browns and 200 two-year-olds which average about 13 to 15 inches long. Most but not all of the stockings take place within the creek's 6 miles of bank decorated with public fishing signs, including 1.9 miles in the Steuben County-Marsh Creek sectors.

In addition to its moderate stocking quota, Cryder Creek holds a fair population of wild brown and brook trout, with most of the "natives" hiding out in undercuts and riffles upstream from Whitesville. Some landowners in this area will grant permission to fish, and some will not. Either way, be sure to ask before you cast.

Although this 20-foot-wide creek does not, at first blush, seem to be a difficult stream to approach and fish, anglers who like to take a long walk upstream or downstream and work their way back to their parked cars will quickly notice steep and occasionally undercut banks. These features are mostly the results of long-term, seasonal floods and erosion. Be careful to avoid deep, loose sand bars, don't be tempted to take any shortcuts, and don't take any chances tripping in tangles of brush or small cave-ins, and other hazards! Such precautions are often merited in streams, such as Cryder Creek, where nightcrawlers and forked-stick rod holders come in handy.

More intimate sections of the creek, downstream from Whitesville, and in particular those stretches with rock and gravel bottoms and the occasional log jam, provide shelter for some nice wild browns and brookies, and you probably won't need to be leaning on your wading stick all the time.

LITTLE GENESEE CREEK

RATING: ★★ (2 stars)

BEST TIME TO FISH: Get them early in the season, before beavers affect the fishery.

BEST METHODS: Use a dropper and tippet-fly rig to prospect with two wet flies at a time.

A fair-size creek, running two- to four-feet deep in quite a few spots and spreading out to approximately 25 or even 30 feet across, the Little Genesee is not a tributary of the regionally renowned Genesee River. Rather, it is part of the Allegheny River watershed. Mother Nature zinged a whole bunch of us on this one, probably with help from a cartographer or a politician who had figured out a way to benefit from such a puzzling misnomer. But as wags have been fond of repeating since Shakespeare's day, a creek by any other name is still a creek.

The Little Genny winds through southwestern Allegany County enroute to its confluence with the mighty Allegany, just a short drive south from the New York-Pennsylvania border. It has some notable assets, including a total of 3.5 miles of public fishing along its banks and a fairly large annual stocking quota, consisting of 2,200 brook trout along with 1,500 yearling browns and 200 two-year-old browns. Fishing is best, in most years, during the first two months of the season, before water temperatures climb to levels intolerable for trout, stocked or wild. The terrain along the creek's banks consist mainly of abandoned oil fields that are gradually filling in with scrub vegetation, first-growth forest tracts and the clusters of suburban dwellings and lawns that are becoming pretty ubiquitous along back roads in New York's Southern Tier counties.

One natural problem that undoubtedly impacts on the water quality in the Little Genesee is beaver-dam building, which leads to silt build-ups, warming water from mid-spring into early autumn at least, and smothering of spawning gravel, to name just a few concerns about *Castor canadensis* and its ways. Trappers and fishermen are natural allies wherever nature's bucktoothed engineers thrive, and may gain the upper hand for a time.

But not for a long time, unfortunately. When you wager on the tenacity of beavers, you really can bet—or lose—the farm.

OTHER ALLEGANY COUNTY TROUT STREAMS

In the spring of the year, hundreds of tiny rills you can clear with running jumps and the few dozen creeks that cannot be bypassed without some careful wading are all licking at their banks. Some of these waters beg to be fished, and others should not be bothered, because their trout populations are depleted and likely will remain that way for years. In this book, readers will find waters that can be fished responsibly, and revisited from time to time without causing injury to a valuable natural resource. Unless special regulations say otherwise, these rivers, creeks and brooks can afford to lose a trout to the creel now and then. But that is not a carte blanche permit from the author or his publisher. Prudent judgement is called for when an angler holds a wild trout in his hands and tries to visualize whether it will look better rising for next week's mayfly hatch or sizzling in a cast-iron frying pan for your mother-in-law's birthday dinner.

Removing a couple of trout from a swift-flowing stream for a special occasion is more commendable than hauling a three-pounder from a sizable creek because you want to show it off to your friends. The creeling of a heavy brown may well give you a bad case of buyer's remorse, and the stream that big boy used to live in won't be the same for months or years to come. Stick with the little fellows, I say, and don't take more than a few 10- or 12-inchers per season from any of those small creeks you might have discovered over the years.

While the final decision is left to the reader, the following Allegany County streams strike me as being sufficiently healthy and populous to give up a trout or two during an annual trout season. If you are personally knowledgeable about any of these creeks, think how many of them are posted "no trespassing" or have had their stream beds turned inside-out by recent floods. Always err on the conservative side if you're not sure how many trout you might glean after a mid-summer rain storm, without causing any harm to the resource. Where posting is heavy, most anglers tend to crowd public fishing areas, instead of knocking on doors to ask permission to fish on private land. That shyness or timidity results in increasing numbers of fish in posted areas and a noticeable decline in catches from public water that doesn't have no-kill or other protective regulations.

Keep track of your successes and failures as you try your luck on unfamiliar waters in Western New York. The data I scrawled on my angler-diary pages for 30-some trout seasons helped me to catch more and bigger trout than I would have netted otherwise. More than once, my successful do-it-yourself quests often began by taking a look at the tributaries of a larger creek or river.

Those readers who jotted down directions to Cryder Creek on a day when the trout of southeastern Allegany County were surprisingly shy wound up salvaging their trip by making a right turn in Whitesville, where Routes 248 and 248A intersect. Due-east of that junction, **Spring Mills Creek** flows along County Road 19. Although there are no designated public fishing areas on the creek, much of the land is not posted. Wild brookies are the only species of trout in this five- to eight-foot-wide stream, and some of them are decent size, up to 10 or 11 inches long. A garden worm is your best bet in this and many other tiny tributaries.

Root Creek and **California Hollow Brook** are two more worthy waters, found in the Bolivar area, about 15 miles southwest of Wellsville. Both are primarily put-and-take creeks, stocked each spring by DEC hatcheries, but are capable of rewarding a diligent angler with a wild brown once in a while. Root Creek links up with Little Genesee Creek in the village of Bolivar. California Hollow, located about 5 miles east of Bolivar via California Hollow Road (also known as County Route 33) has about three-quarters of a mile of public fishing near the intersection of Route 33 and 18. Considering the small dimensions of California Hollow, its recent stocking rate of 800 browns each spring seems quite ample.

Trout streams, like other natural resources, have their ups and downs in the long term. The "ups" result from intensive habitat improvement, increased stocking programs and special regulations aimed at improving overall population levels and surpassing other management goals. Down-periods, of course, can be attributed to industrial or agriculture-related pollution as well as stream channel impoundments and temperatures that soar above levels suitable for trout survival.

Honeoye Creek, which flows along Route 33 and the Pennsylvania border between Alma and South Bolivar, is a good example of the "ups" and "downs." Beaver damage has been horrific at times, but the creek is reputed to hold some large brown trout, even in or near ponded areas. Although no public access can be found along the creek, the angler who happens to be in the general area to do a bit of fishing has nothing to lose by asking for permission to give Honeoye Creek a try.

Three more creeks that add many gallons of cold water to the Genesee River near Wellsville are on my itinerary whenever I happen to be in the area. They are **Vandermark Creek**, **Fulmer Valley Creek** and **Ford Brook**.

Vandermark Creek is about 10 to 15 feet wide for most of its steep-gradient run along Vandermark Road in the town of Ward. It is home to wild browns and brook trout and early in the season stocked browns are caught there, too. However, it is rather heavily posted, and touring anglers should seek permission to trespass with rod in hand.

Fulmer Valley Creek is a 10- to 12-foot-wide tributary of Chenunda Creek, which is in turn an important feeder of the Genesee River. It flows along Fulmer Valley Road and enters Chenunda Creek about a mile downstream (west) of Hallsport.

Fulmer Valley Creek has moderate populations of wild brook and brown trout. Most are under 10 inches long, but since browns in Chenunda Creek seem to be of a larger average size today than they were a few years ago, it would not be surprising if some bigger browns showed up in future electrofishing surveys. Such trends might be short-lived, however, because Fulmer Valley Creek has few deep pools or undercuts to hide shy browns from herons and other predators.

Ford Brook enters the Genesee River from its west side, about midway between Stannards and the Route 29 crossing at York Corners. The most recent electrofishing survey of the brook, carried out in 2009 at three locations, showed the presence of wild browns and brookies. The natives were more numerous, but the browns were more impressive, size-wise. One brown stretched the tape to 18½ inches, and another one measured 12½ inches. Several small tributaries held wild brook trout, including a couple which were between nine and 10 inches long.

Like so many other very rural brooks in southern Allegany County, Ford Brook and its branches could benefit from additional public access. Until that need is met, anglers will have to knock on doors and use their sharpest diplomatic skills to gain permission to fish.

Dodge Creek is, in the main, an April-May fishery. It hooks up with the Allegheny River in the Cattaraugus County village of Portville, and it is stocked with 2,200 hatchery-born brook trout and 200 two-year-old browns in April. A second stocking, consisting of 1,500 yearling browns, takes place in May. Summer fishing is slow, for the most part, because water temperatures are marginal for trout after late May or early June. Stocking sites are scattered for about 8 miles from Temple Street in Portville upstream to the hamlet of West Clarksville. The creek is big enough, about 25 feet across, to easily accommodate fly fishers.

CHAPTER FIVE

Erie and Niagara Counties

In the process of planning and writing this book, the publisher and I noticed right away that most of the good trout streams in Western New York are found in the Southern Tier (Chautauqua, Allegany, Cattaraugus) or in Wyoming County. Among them, those four counties can lay claim to more than 50 brooks, creeks and rivers which have the cold water and bank cover that are required to support wild or stocked trout.

Because *Trout Streams of Western New York* is specifically about inland trout waters, and not the famed tributaries of Lakes Ontario or Erie, we necessarily left out several streams which have superb fishing for fall-run brown trout. Another volume in the catalog of Burford Books, written by freelance author Spider Rybaak, does a great job of covering these Great Lakes tribs from the traveling angler's viewpoint. It's called, appropriately, *Fishing the Great Lakes of New York*. Its scope includes tips on finding, accessing and fishing tributaries such as Eighteen-Mile Creek, in Newfane. Look for it at your favorite bookstores or order direct from Burford Books, in Ithaca, New York.

Meanwhile, here's a helpful chapter of advice on another fishing secret, i.e., the unknown and overlooked inland trout streams of Erie County. As with the other counties covered in Part I of this book, the qualifying trout streams will be rated according to a "star system" that runs from a single star up to five stars.

Okay. Please permit the author to take a couple of deep breaths. That feels better. If you live and fish in the Buffalo-Niagara Falls area, you should be able to guess where I'm going with this chapter. I've consulted with other sources and confirmed my belief that Erie County has only half a dozen genuine inland trout streams, and Niagara County has *zero*. That's right, zero. Zip, nada, none. On the other hand—and I'm about to stir up a hornet's nest if I'm not careful—Niagara County residents can justly boast of having some of the best brown-trout fishing in the United States, if not the world. I won't argue that. Unfortunately, virtually all of this trout action occurs between late September and late November, when tens of thousands of Lake Ontario brownies are ready to ingest the eggs laid by king and coho salmon as well as those deposited in riffle gravel by their own species. These fish often weigh more than 15 pounds, but because they are not year-round residents of the aforementioned spawning creeks, they aren't part of any inland fishery, either.

That makes me sound like a bespectacled bean counter and nit-picker, but for consistency's sake I am going to hold the line against covering Eighteen-Mile Creek, Twelve Mile Creek, Keg Creek and a couple of other seasonal trout fisheries in this volume.

Erie County is a different breed, as it contains several inland trout streams, and a couple of those are of outstanding quality. Read 'em and weep, if you've never given the following waters a thorough test.

HOSMER BROOK

RATING: ★★★★ (4 stars)

BEST TIME TO FISH: After a summer shower, because the brook clears faster than most streams in the area and its trout keep on feeding when the others have quit.

BEST METHOD: A tough call, but I'd pick a small minnow-imitating bait, such as a Yozuri lure, that can be maneuvered with care through toppled branches and other hiding places, ever so slowly.

Electrofishing Hosmer Brook is one of those "jobs" that hard-working fisheries biologists and Trout Unlimited volunteers line up for in due season. Before and after Labor Day, Region 9 survey crews have plenty

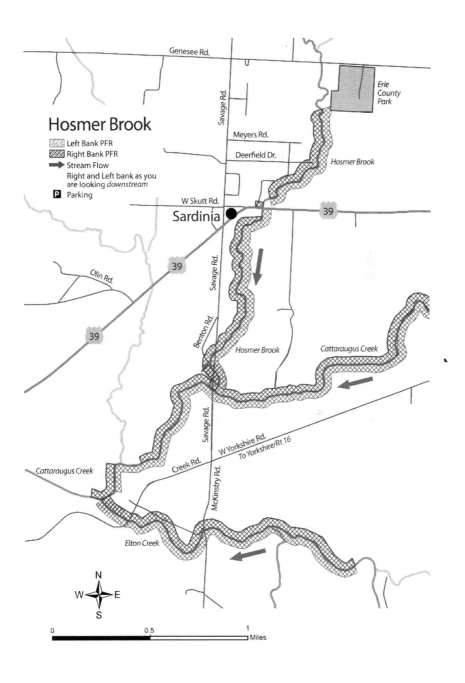

Hosmer Brook

Left Bank PFR
Right Bank PFR
Stream Flow
Right and Left bank as you
are looking *downstream*
P Parking

Genesee Rd.

Savage Rd.

Erie
County
Park

Meyers Rd.

Deerfield Dr.

Hosmer Brook

W Skutt Rd.

Sardinia

39

39

Olin Rd.

39

Savage Rd.

Benton Rd.

Hosmer Brook

Cattaraugus Creek

Savage Rd.

W Yorkshire Rd.

To Yorkshire/Rt 16

Cattaraugus Creek

Creek Rd.

McKinstry Rd.

Elton Creek

N
W E
S

0   0.5   1
Miles

of opportunities to do head counts and scale samples, but none are more coveted than Hosmer, which is called Sardinia Brook by local anglers. The creek is full of brown trout, most in the eight- to 11-inch range, but now and then somebody—a fishermen as likely as a fisheries scientist—will catch a plump 15-incher. Rainbows in Hosmer Brook aren't nearly as abundant as the browns, but the stream holds many eight- to nine-inchers and the electrofishers collect specimens that cover the 11- or 12-inch marks on the DEC measuring board.

The year 1993 was the last time Hosmer Brook was stocked. Since then, the brook has been assayed by electrofishers half a dozen times, and the survey has always turned up good to excellent numbers of trout, especially for a stream that's barely eight- to 15-feet wide. Browns seem to rule the watershed, even though catch rates for rainbow trout are higher. That is often the case where browns and rainbows jockey for coveted feeding and resting locations. Browns have the muscles and the minds to take over streams, if needed, but rainbows don't have quite what it takes. During the 2007 population check, state crews esti-mated the biomass of adult brown trout in Hosmer Brook at about 52 pounds per acre, or approximately 404 fish per linear mile. By way of comparison, the same parts of the brook (three sites chosen, including the Route 39 section in Sardinia) contained 17 pounds of rainbows per acre and 295 of the same species per linear mile.

Yellow-bellied browns and gorgeous rainbows with parr marks showing along their lateral lines are your target trout in Hosmer Brook, and you can get your share by dapping streamer flies (the black Wooly Bugger is a good one) or flipping and retrieving diminutive Yozuri-type stickbaits or perhaps a Panther Martin spinner with a black body and a gold-colored spinner blade.

Route 39, also known as the Springville-Sardinia Highway, provides a direct route to the excellent fishing in Hosmer Brook. Anglers can pick up the road in Springville, then follow it in a generally east-north-east direction to Sardinia. Mayflies, caddis and other aquatic insects are present in sufficiently high numbers to attract many early- and mid-season fly fishers. However, because anglers hammer this stream as soon as the spring weather permits, I would advise folks who live more than an hour's drive from Hosmer Brook to take a chance by scheduling visits in the last couple of days in May and the first week to 10 days of the same month. That's earlier than most of the regulars would recommend, but you will have plenty of blue-winged olives and blue quills to keep you alert, and the early-May hatches will also attract considerable attention from the pound- to pound-and-a-half browns that cause most of the swirling rises seen on this stream.

Another good rule comes to mind: the wilder the trout you encounter, the more likely it is that you will be able to tease some beauties to the surface. Instead of stocking your fly boxes with perfect mayfly imitations, try stirring up the big ones by drifting an Ausable Wulff or any similar patterns that just look "buggy," ask the shop owners for a few local patterns that haven't been discovered yet.

Finally, don't rely solely on big size 10s and 12s. The trout here in Hosmer Brook do like big bites, but if the mayflies and other bugs coming off the surface are mostly size 16s and 18s, those are the ones you will need to have at the end of your leader. And, speaking of leaders, anglers of sound mind and body will find tippet sections of 5X are adequate during April and May, but 6X could get you more strikes in the late spring and summer. Many of today's high-tech monofilament leaders have 6X diameters (.005) which have breaking points of 4 or 5 pounds of pressure. You'd have to try very hard to break off a 2-pound brown trout on such tackle.

Access to Hosmer Brook, by Western New York standards, is very good, if not excellent. The DEC has its public fishing markers along a mile and a half of stream banks, and there is an unofficial, privately-owned pull off, at the junction pool where the brook joins upper Cattaraugus Creek. To get to it, drive into Sardinia and go south along Buffalo Street. You will cross the brook twice, and then you will see the DEC signs just ahead. This entire stretch has good fishing, but it is lined with thick brush and you should expect some difficult casting, at times.

Fishing in the upper reaches of Hosmer Brook is also inspiring, from the Route 39 bridge to Genesee Road and beyond. However, you should come prepared for some bush-whacking. The stream winds back and forth around dense clumps of willows, which makes for tricky walking as well as challenging fishing. You will find a couple of fairly open meadows, but the main hazard, other than those boot-grabbing

Author wades at base of a spillway on Hosmer Brook, in Sardinia.

willows, is the slick clay which is plainly visible along certain stretches of the brook. Use a wading staff and move very cautiously as you negotiate this part of the stream. The fishing can be very rewarding but a bad fall might ruin your trip if you hurry when you shouldn't.

Hosmer Brook is often described as a suburban trout fishery, but that characterization is a bit misleading. The stream flows through the small village of Sardinia, but is about 10 miles east of Springville via Route 39. It's also an easy, 25-minute drive south from East Aurora, via Routes 16 and 39. I personally think of this beautiful fishing hole in the southeast corner of Erie County as a rather remote and relaxing spot—but more "rural" than "suburban." Whatever I or any other fishing writer chooses to call it, Hosmer Brook is sometimes crowded with anglers from Buffalo and its suburbs, for the obvious reason that it has very good trout fishing.

SPRING BROOK

RATING: ★★★ (3 stars)

BEST TIME TO FISH: When a summer thunderstorm washes fresh food into the creek, be there or be square.

BEST METHOD: Match a post-storm "hatch" of scuds, bugs and cranefly larvae imitations. These are some of the critters washed into the water by storms.

Seeing Spring Brook flow under bridges and through back yards in eastern Erie County is like getting a free ticket for the culture clash on the verge of erupting in those parts of Western New York which have thriving populations of migratory steelhead as well as resident brown, rainbow and brook trout.

I know the opera isn't over until the fat lady sings, but she is already spraying her throat and chirping "me-me-me-me-me-me-me" in the offices of DEC decision-makers. If I had to place a bet right now, I would wager that the state of New York and other government entities who have to say "yes" to make it happen will soon give the final go-aheads for breaching the Scoby Dam in Springville. If it happens, steelhead now blocked from spawning further upstream will gradually or perhaps quickly turn their noses into the current and Cattaraugus Creek steelies will find their way to dozens of new spawning grounds, in the tributaries as well as the main stream. Wild browns, rainbows and brook trout which have made these upstream redoubts their home, sweet home for many decades may then be forced to fight off steelhead that out-weigh them by a factor of five-, 10 or even 20 to one, or turn around and find some better place to live and reproduce.

There's no better place to get a feel for the magnitude of the trout vs. trout battle than the village of Springville. It is the place where steelheads will stay put or continue upstream in search of new spawning gravel. The big fish will be easy to find, as their forms flash through riffles and pools. It will not be so easy for the many small trout, who do not know they are on the verge of being displaced by much larger relatives.

Blowing up the dam that has kept steelhead and smaller species of trout separated for many years will be a fateful and worrisome decision, when it is made. Well into the planning stages, we do not know which streams are most likely to be impacted, but the experts are unanimous in their belief that there will be no new dam—*ever*—to replace the one that's going to be carefully smacked down by a wrecking ball. The researchers monitoring the steelhead expansion do not seem to have any doubt that the big 'bows charging up the creek past Springville in years ahead will be rough and tough enough to go into the very head-waters of Cattaraugus Creek and its feeders, if that's what their instincts tell them to do.

One of the few places that offer a sliver of optimism to fans of small-stream fishing in this sobering scenario is Spring Brook. A stream that averages about 10 feet wide, Spring Brook is one of a very few waters in the western part of the state which is dominated by bigger-than-average, totally wild brook trout, or, as I prefer to call them, "natives."

The brook I'm talking about is a gorgeous stream that winds through the village of Springville. And yes, that's the same Springville where Scoby Dam, ultimately and literally, will stand or fall when the DEC goes beyond the point of no return—or decides to leave Cattaraugus Creek and its tributaries alone. It's the epicenter of the big debate, in other words.

And you won't believe what Spring Brook looks like. It reminds me of the many spring-fed, so-called "limestone creeks" that pop up in central and south central Pennsylvania. The little streams I am thinking of, like the Letort Spring Run near Carlisle, Big Spring near Newville,

A pretty rainbow trout caught in Clear Creek, near Arcade.

and parts of Yellow Breeches Creek in and around Boiling Springs, are famous for their wary trout and crystalline currents. They have thick, instream beds of watercress and elodea, which serve as habitat and feeding grounds for resident brown, brook and rainbow trout.

Best of all, those Pennsylvania creeks—and New York's Spring Brook, too—run clear as a bell even after a day-long downpour. One can fish such waters day after day, throughout the season, and with confidence—for the simple reason that the angler can see most of the fish he's after, as long as he wears a good pair or polarized lenses and keeps still between casts.

Spring Brook stands out from the crowd in that its prime section, located immediately upstream from a 12-foot-high, impassable barrier above South Buffalo Street, at last look held only brook trout—all of them wild.

On July 17, 2006, DEC workers and volunteers collected fish at three sites along the brook. This survey focused on the Upper Brook, i.e., above the South Buffalo barrier. The three sites chosen produced a total of 31 adult natives, including one 10.6 inches long. Seven of the 31 captured brookies were longer than nine inches. In general, survey participants were pleased with the number of fish they measured and also with the quality of trout habitat in Spring Brook. One potentially serious problem with the stream should be mentioned. That's the siltation in the brook above the spillway. It seems to be the result of beaver activity in the headwaters and unstable soil in the community park.

Fishermen should be warned that, despite its obvious potential for recreation, Spring Creek has no public fishing area. The one possible exception is the small park above South Buffalo Street. You should ask permission of land owners before rigging up.

Other Erie County Trout Streams include some with very limited access, such as waters flowing through the Seneca Indian reservation and others which are heavily posted by individual land owners. Readers who frequently fish for steelhead on parts of Cattaraugus Creek below the Springville (Scoby) dam know they are required to obtain a current-season fishing license from the Seneca Nation before they wet a line in tribal streams. Anglers who buy licenses from the Senecas should ask, in particular, about the **Main Branch of Clear Creek,** which is off Taylor Hollow Road just north of Gowanda. It is reputed to be the home of some fair-size brook trout. The main attraction in the 20-foot-wide tributary, however, is the big run of steelhead from Lake Erie and Cattaraugus Creek in September, October and November.

Another you might ask about is the **North Branch of Clear Creek**. It has, along with the expected steelhead, a fishable number of wild rainbows that might tape out at a respectable 12 or 13 inches. The North Branch also crosses Taylor Hollow Road. By the way, the tributaries of the entire Cattaraugus Creek watershed can be fished with hip boots in most circumstances. You can leave your XX-L size chest waders at home, for once!

Coon Brook, which is a hop, skip and short drive in your fishing car from the two branches of Clear Creek, is accessible from Zoar Valley Road—the one leading to the state-owned Zoar Valley Wildlife Management Area. It's only about six feet wide in most places, and has ample gravel for trout spawning. If you hit it just right, you have decent odds of getting stream-bred brown, rainbow and (rarely) brook trout. These fish don't get very big, as a rule, but anglers fishing the Coon Brook for 10-inchers should brace themselves for much larger trout during local snow-melts and other runoff periods. Sometimes, locals say, browns living in Cattaraugus Creek will make a bold charge upstream, riding swollen currents that make normally impassable spots relatively easy to clear.

Because Coon Brook has a substantial number of juvenile rainbows in its lower reaches, the DEC advises anglers to catch and release in the stream, and that policy seems reasonable to me, as well.

Not all trout fisheries need to be subject to complicated regulations, and some get lots of use after the hatchery trucks come calling to sportsmen along the accessible segments of urban streams.

Among the waters in Erie County that depend on the state fish farms to maintain put-and-take action close to home, the **East Branch of Cazenovia Creek** and **Ellicott Creek** are great for families which want to initiate youngsters in their favorite sport. Of course, the participants don't cause any harm by putting a couple of fat browns on a stringer, either. The East Branch is stocked in the spring with around 3,600 yearling "catchables" and another 300 or so two-year-olds. Most of the hatchery grads are unloaded between Holland and South Wales, and the 20-foot-wide creek is very popular, in part because most local land owners admit visitors without much hassle. Informal pull-offs are common along Route 16 and most bridge crossings.

Although most of its recreation opportunities are derived from regular stocking programs, the East Branch is known to produce a few wild browns, too. The best way to put your bait, lure or fly in front of such fish is to focus your effort on the headwaters of the Caz, above Holland; or perhaps try the deep pools south of the same village via Route 16.

Ellicott Creek, located in the village of Williamson, is strictly put-and-take, as DEC survey records do not reveal the presence of any wild trout. However, the state does plant about 1,125 rainbow trout annually, most of them winding up in a village park that straddles the community's Main Street. The season on this conveniently located suburban stream is usually cut short in late May or early June due rising water temperatures.

One more trout fishery in Erie County that has a strong following among urban anglers is **Cayuga Creek**, which flows through Lancaster. The 50-foot-wide stream is stocked in spring time in Lake Como Park with about 3,150 rainbows. Unfortunately, rising temperatures threaten trout in the park by the end of June. Consequently, most of the stocking takes place during April.

CHAPTER SIX

Wyoming County

Did we save the best for last? Wyoming County indisputably has some of the finest trout fishing in Western New York, and possibly the entire state. If I were looking for a great way to wrap up the first part of this guide book, I could do far worse than to express my deep appreciation for Wiscoy Creek and its all-wild population of brilliantly colored brown trout. I was tugged in that direction at first, but worried I might be jumping the gun. Would-a, could-a, should-a, I suppose. . . . (We trout fishermen can be awfully ambivalent at times.)

Not too long ago, the Wiscoy was pretty much in a class of its own. Anglers from throughout the Northeast knew where it was, what species it held, and the fisheries-management blueprint that could nurture more than 2,500 adult trout per linear mile.

Sadly, things have changed, and more than a tiny bit. Although Wiscoy Creek's population figures are still better than most, and the Department of Environmental Conservation, for now, is sticking by its policy of not stocking the stream, the short-term outlook is not all warm and fuzzy. In truth, the creek may be in for some rough times, for a while. Region 9's top trout researcher, Scott Cornett, issued a report on the previous year's electrofishing and diary program, dated January, 2016, that suggests Wiscoy Creek may be at a historic crossroads.

Meanwhile, more than a few anglers would be willing to make the case that Wiscoy is still the sort of trout stream which can make a veteran angler drool all over his wader tops, and the rest of Wyoming County has several other outstanding creeks and brooks that I have fished before and am extremely interested in trying again.

But in these days when anglers have festering concerns, like birds that prey heavily on trout, and mega-problems such as global climate change, we probably all have too much on our plates to argue about which rivers and counties are truly the best of the best. We should lock arms, figuratively, and stand united to deal with our environmental challenges, one by one.

At least, I think so.

WISCOY CREEK

RATING: ★★★★ (4 stars)
BEST TIME TO FISH: Memorial Day weekend, when the Green Drakes
    hatch and their spinners, the Coffin Flies, fill the skies at twilight.
BEST METHODS: Take an afternoon nap, but set the alarm to make sure
    you're ready to fish the appropriate dry flies until well after dark.

A few years earlier, that four-star rating you just blinked at and assumed to be a typographical error would have triggered some nasty comments, possibly even one or two addressed to me on official DEC stationery. Yep, somebody affiliated with the state's environmental management outfit would be wondering why anybody would snub Wiscoy Creek, when "almost everyone" in the DEC "knew" that stream flowing through beautiful farm country was the best trout water in Region 9—bar none.

In fact, the almost universally praised creek was slipping a little, although it would be neither correct nor fair to suggest that fisheries management practices had much to do with it. The fishing was in decline, or at least that's how many anglers saw it. They began asking the DEC administrators to "do something" although they did not always have a notion of what, exactly *could* be done.

What sort of changes have we been talking about? Cornett, Region 9's trout biologist *extraordinaire*, had tracked the ups and downs of stream fisheries throughout Western New York throughout his 26-year career, but the wave of worries over the fate of Wiscoy Creek was unlike

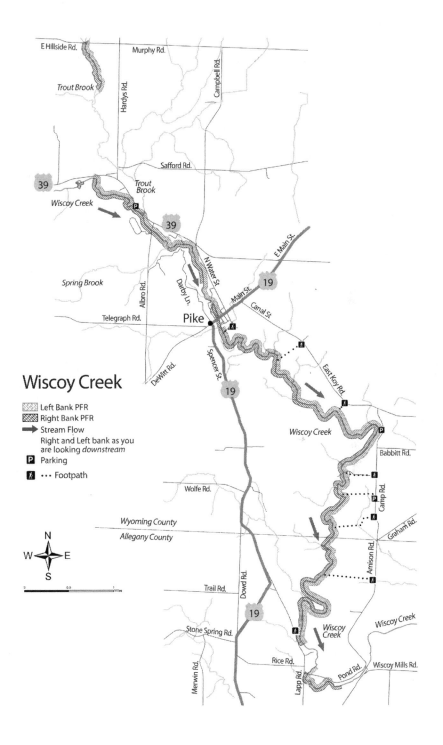

E Hillside Rd.

Murphy Rd.

Campbell Rd.

Hardys Rd.

Trout Brook

Safford Rd.

39

Trout
Brook

Wiscoy Creek

39

N Water St.

E Main St.

Spring Brook

Albro Rd.

Darby Ln.

Main St.

Canal St.

19

Telegraph Rd.

Pike

DeWitt Rd.

Spencer St.

19

East Koy Rd.

Wiscoy Creek

Wiscoy Creek

▨ Left Bank PFR
▧ Right Bank PFR
➡ Stream Flow
Right and Left bank as you
are looking *downstream*
🅿 Parking
🚶 ••• Footpath

Babbitt Rd.

Camp Rd.

Wolfe Rd.

Graham Rd.

Wyoming County
Allegany County

Amison Rd.

N
W ◆ E
S

Dowd Rd.

Trail Rd.

19

Stone Spring Rd.

Wiscoy
Creek

Wiscoy Creek

Merwin Rd.

Rice Rd.

Lapp Rd.

Pond Rd.

Wiscoy Mills Rd.

anything else he had ever seen. Perhaps it would be helpful to readers if some of the issues raised with regard to the stream could be posted for discussion—starting with this one, in boldface type:

The trout just aren't there anymore. Perhaps the most common complaint is the one that suggests trout populations have shriveled to the point that only the most skillful of today's anglers can catch them. The corollary of that assumption is, if we can't catch any of the Wiscoy's wild trout, maybe the DEC will just have to start stocking the creek again. That is what some folks call a "non-starter."

The creek hasn't been stocked for more than 50 years, but even during this puzzling time, electrofishing crews can still put some gorgeous trout on the stream bank. Last summer, for instance, state workers visited 10 sites on the creek, and used their electric wands to check out the fish living in the neighborhood. The bad news was that, of the 10 sites surveyed in 2015, eight had their worst research catches, yet. Despite the general down-trend, Cornett and the rest of the Region 9 trout-counting team shocked about 1,156 browns per mile during last year's expedition, plus some very healthy "natives" in or very near Trout Brook. The last-named stream, although thickly over-grown, is famous for its wild, pot-bellied brookies.

Something has happened to our aquatic insect hatches. Now, this one is a true classic. Everyone seemed to have the opinion that hatches of the fluttering Green Drakes and their spinners with the waxy white abdomens and the mottled wings have been "off" for several years. The big-time fly fishers living in the vicinity of the creek said the hatch was not the only bug worth showing a fly or two, but the once-reliable drakes no longer could be counted on; and when they finally showed up on the creek's surface, they were not as thick as they used to be. My reaction to those moans and groans, after fishing several Catskill rivers which are notorious for their heavy but enigmatic hatches, is "Welcome to *my* world, Buddy!"

And, no, I don't think a couple of sub-par mayfly hatches, or even a trout season that's packed with such events, should discourage beginners or veterans from planning do-overs in the near future. The bugs might make a comeback, you know.

Wiscoy trout don't get as big as the fish in some other streams, like its neighbor, East Koy Creek, for example.

Actually, that used to be the case, but not any longer. The highlight of the electrofishing work done in 2015 was the capture of a 22½-inch wild brown, the largest one on record from Wiscoy Creek surveys. Impressed? I sure was, especially when the state team reported that six of the 10 survey sites served up at least one wild brown that measured 18 inches or more.

For many years, Wiscoy Creek was widely reputed to be producing many brown trout in the 12- to 14-inch class, a few of 15- to 16-inches, and almost no 17- to 18-inch beauties, let alone the occasional 20-inch-plus whales like those that made other western New York waters famous. (Ischua Creek around Franklinville and Clear Creek near Arcade come to mind here.)

Lately, Wiscoy Creek's problems do not appear to result from having too many trout. Instead, area experts think the stream could use a lot more eight- to 13-inchers. That size range applies to at least two and perhaps three separate year-classes of trout, and it explains why DEC experts were concerned when electrofishing data indicated browns of that size were essentially all gone from the creek. The lingering question is, how did this happen, and the second issue is, what can we do to prevent it from happening again. We will have to pin the blame on somebody or something; that is for sure.

Some of the potential villains in this drama could be dismissed quite easily. All we need to determine is which animals in this neighborhood are big enough to hunt and capture trout that are more than a foot long.

So you are blaming those accursed birds for killing too many trout?

What birds, specifically? I know from just looking around every now and then that great blue herons, ospreys, and many other birds—from kingfishers to bald eagles—like to stand silently at water's edge or dive bomb from above when their stomachs say it's supper time. But we also need to be aware that an assortment of other animals—including river otters, mink and beavers, to name just a few—can also do damage to a local trout population.

Fishing nymphs on Wiscoy Creek near Bliss.

The junction pool where Trout Brook flows into Wiscoy Creek.

What about disease? Didn't the state hatchery system have some problems a few years ago?

Yes, as a matter of fact, there was a serious outbreak of whirling disease at the Caledonia hatchery quite a while back, and another problem at the Rome fish lab. The most interesting thing about those situations was that they were not followed by any epidemic beyond the hatchery gates. Many anglers have forgotten that the outbreak of whirling disease which occurred a few years back pummeled hatchery rainbows but apparently never impacted New York's brown trout to any appreciable degree, in or out of our hatchery network.

So it really is the damned birds, right?

Not necessarily, but I can see you have your mind made up, so I'll tell you what I think. Some in the DEC hierarchy have been leaning this way, lately, but only because the pertinent hypothesis is logical. I prefer to sell it as an example of good, old, outdoorsy common sense.

It has been at least 10 years and probably more like 15 or 20 since I last went hunting for common mergansers, which are also known as "lawn darts" in my wise-cracking circle of friends. The big ducks with the dark rust-colored heads, long necks and stiff but pointy bills are half-seriously said to be just right, when frozen solid, for use in a certain back-yard party game. Putting that back-handed compliment aside for a moment, one must admit mergansers are very efficient at what nature intended them to do, namely, catch fish and eat their catch. Further, many anglers have reported increased sightings of mergansers in and around Wiscoy Creek, especially in the spring and early summer, when mother mergansers are frequently observed leading their offspring hither and yon. After a few such lessons, the young birds routinely line up and dive, each in turn, as if they were cogs in some deadly fish-eating machine.

Avian predators that aren't able to feed cooperatively in some circumstances can find it that much harder to score a fish or two at meal time. I remember watching a common loon diving, over and over, in Clark's Creek, a gin-clear stream near Harrisburg, PA. Johnny Weissmuller ("Me Tarzan, You Jane") had nothing on that bird, as a swimmer. However, the loon was stymied by the natural obstacles in its path, such as roots protruding from the bank of the creek, and midstream rocks. That afternoon, I was not the only fellow who went home without hooking a single trout.

Another flying fisherman with a bum rap is the hated cormorant, which establishes large breeding and nesting colonies on Lake Ontario and elsewhere. Cormorants usually, although not always, stick to open water and focus on abundant prey species, such as round gobies, yellow perch and gizzard shad.

Getting back to mergansers, they are not at all averse to eating trout in the eight- to 13-inch range. They seem to fish cooperatively, especially with their own offspring, and they are rapid flyers which means they can quickly move from one fishing spot to another as circumstances dictate. However, mergansers (like loons) can be frustrated by a lack of visibility or the presence of downed trees and other obstacles once they have gone underwater.

Adding to the mystery in this case, Cornett is personally satisfied that the Wiscoy has not sustained any habitat losses that could make it a snap for mergansers to target trout in the stream. Other anglers have suggested the destruction of some log cribbing-type shelters in the 1980s and '90s reduced the depth of some man-made pools and made it easier to herd trout from one bird to another, but Cornett does not think the damage was on a large scale.

"As a crew member on all Wiscoy fish sampling since 1991," he said, "I have a fairly good feel for changes over time at our (electrofishing) sites."

At this writing, DEC fisheries personnel still have a lot of research to complete, and they have not yet determined, for a fact, that mergansers or any other predators are to blame, wholly or in part for the plainly reduced numbers of trout in Wiscoy Creek and its tributaries.

In other words, stay tuned! And, whatever else you may be planning to do with your trout rod this season, don't leave that precious stick to gather dust at home, for Wiscoy still harbors plenty of wild brown trout. They will need an occasional workout, and you readers can supply that.

Wiscoy Creek flows 13 miles through southern Wyoming County before crossing the border into Allegany County, southeast of the village of Pike. It has about 9.4 miles of public fishing rights, enroute. Posting is moderate upstream from Bliss but light elsewhere along the creek. Between the mouth of Trout Brook and the border crossing you will have to look hard to spot any "keep out" warnings. Fishermen have helped their own cause in Wyoming County by picking up after themselves and others, and by simply being courteous to any locals they happen to encounter.

Keeping up those good relations between sportsman and land owner should be one of the top priorities of angler-conservationists in western New York. That's especially true when the topic of discussion is whatever is going on within the high-water marks along Wiscoy Creek—which I, personally, expect to remain one of the top three or four trout streams in DEC Region 9. Following well-maintained highways into the heart of Wyoming County and then checking out country roads and angler parking areas and footpaths, we can take notes and perhaps come up with a few digital camera images, too. If you have the discipline to leave your rod in the car while you undertake your first look around Wiscoy's pretty bends and plunge pools and such, well, you're a better man than I am. I got my first glimpses of Wiscoy Creek's potential back in the days of President Reagan, and it was a case of love at first sight. I fished mostly with buggy nymph patterns during that initial visit, both upstream and down from the confluence of Trout Brook and Wiscoy Creek. The wood, rock and wire stream-improvement devices were intact then, although they would be seriously damaged by flood waters a couple of years later, and the dark undercuts in that area of the stream hid many foot-long browns, as I recall.

These days, the habitat (and the actual fishing) above Bliss is better in some spots and worse in others, but I suspect one can say that about most trout waters, without fear of inaccuracy or exaggeration.

In Wiscoy Creek's headwaters, including the upper end of the North Branch of Wiscoy Creek and Trout Brook near Pike, anglers should wear hip boots, as the water is about 10- to 15 feet across in most spots, and between one- and three-feet deep. The bottom is gravel and cobble-rock-covered and not particularly difficult to wade, although a staff with a rubber tip on it can help you maintain your balance if you find a slick spot.

The main channel of the creek, as well as the North Branch, can be considered brown trout water all the way, although if you fish in the vicinity of Trout Brook regularly, you are bound to catch a native brookie now and then. Natives and browns both fare well in Trout Brook itself, but size-wise, browns have the edge, topping out at around 18 inches in recent surveys by the DEC. You should not expect to catch natives longer than nine or 10 inches long in the brook, although I have heard tales of foot-long specimens here. Access to Trout Brook is easy— if you are only interested in making a couple of casts within sight of the traffic whizzing by on Route 39. As you push your way through the tangles that arch across Trout Brook, you may find yourself checking your watch, swatting at mosquitoes and trying to come up with an excuse to head elsewhere. Yes, the going is really *that* tough, and no, I'm not kidding. Trout Brook has some nice fish but you will earn every single hook-up you get when you try to actually catch something there.

In its great years, such as those experienced by many of today's "old-timers" during the 1980s and 1990s, Wiscoy Creek regulars didn't always do battle with lean and hungry 18-inch brown trout. Selective memory might give such an impression, but in truth a 16-inch-long brownie was a real trophy until a few short years ago. Since the 2010s or thereabout, more two- to three-pound browns than ever were recorded by electrofishers, but numbers of 10- or 12-inchers simultaneously dropped. Hardly a coincidence, wouldn't you agree? While more research is needed to confirm or refute expert opinions and hypotheses, I am waiting for the fisheries unit reports that will spread the blame around for the decline in numbers of eating-size trout. As a couple of my relatives use to say when ideas abounded but proof was lacking, "We will see what we will see."

Meanwhile, there is no reason at all why trout fishermen should not continue to enjoy Wiscoy Creek, inarguably one of the most valuable sources of recreation in New York.

Before shifting gears a bit and turning our focus to the creek's pair of high-quality tributaries, you readers are entitled to a run-down on Wiscoy Creek's main stem, starting with the junction pool area. Whether you set out from points east or west, you certainly will make your final approach to the stream via Route 39, and will probably make your first eyeball inspection as you pull into a traffic rest stop at Pike Five Corners. The landmark here can't be missed, for the Trout Brook road sign is clearly visible between the parking spot and the short bridge spanning the brook. Fishing can be very good at the junction, although in all honesty it was a lot better before downpours ruined half a dozen stream-improvement structures in the area during the 1990s. However, wading is difficult in the junction hole, and before you get stuck in dense brush or something, I would advise you to take a walk up and down the road to mentally note locations where a fisherman of your age, experience and good sense can get in and out of the water without taking a tumble.

Before I highlight several of the better fishing areas along Wiscoy Creek, it might be helpful to identify the special regulations area on the stream. From a marked access sign which is securely pounded into the stream bank a half mile upstream from the East Hillside Road bridge to another sign at a parking area a half mile downstream—one mile overall—the creek is open to fishing year-round, on a catch-and-release basis. Only flies or artificial lures may be used on this No-Kill

Author nymph-fishing Wiscoy Creek in Wyoming County, near the mouth of tributary Trout Brook.

section. Although heavily vegetated in spots, and barely 10 feet wide on average, this section is full of six- to 14 inch brown trout and is especially interesting to fly fishers because it has some heavy hatches of aquatic bugs, including Hendricksons in early May, Green Drakes lasting about a week starting on or about Memorial Day, and swarms of size-24 Trico mayflies most mornings from the Fourth of July through August.

Outside of the Hillside Road no-kill, fly-fishers want to keep track of two other sets of special rules. First, in the parts of the creek that are not within the no-kill, it is permissible to fish from April 1–October 15 (the regular trout season dates). There, an individual angler may creel up to three trout a day, provided they are at least 10 inches long. Also, from Oct. 16 through March 31, fishing is allowed on a no-kill basis only, using artificial lures or flies.

Some of the best dry-fly fishing in the creek, year-in, year-out, can be enjoyed by walking and wading from the tail of the junction down to the dam in the Fireman's Park. You might think the brown trout that rule most of the Wiscoy Creek watershed would share space with at least a few dozen wild brookies in the swirling runs and gravel-bottomed pools and smooth runs east of Trout Brook, but truthfully it is unusual to encounter any natives in the spot. Most likely, the brookies sense they have a good thing going for them in the tributary and just leave well enough alone. The browns in this section, i.e., from the junction into the village of Pike, average about a foot long but these days 18-inchers are not uncommon. Because the water is comparatively smooth-flowing and roughly knee-deep in most areas, I'd call it close to perfect for surface fishing, especially when the drakes are hatching. Streamer fishing is promising after a moderate to heavy thunderstorm has soaked the hay fields and woods along the stream banks, but if you would like to connect with some really nice fish, try casting up and across with a black-and-gold Panther Martin. Crank like hell as soon as the lure hits the water. For reasons I'm not sure of, slow-moving spinners in Wiscoy Creek attract mostly small browns, but big blades provoke some vicious strikes.

As you follow your map downstream through Pike, marked angler footpaths and designated parking areas lead to some 30 to 40-feet-wide bend pools and choppy riffles, all of which shelter 14- to 16-inch browns and, I suspect, a fair number of even larger trout. If you desire a memorable outing in this section of Wiscoy Creek, which runs along East Koy Road, Camp Road and, finally, Lapp Road, bring some weighted nymphs and keep good track of where you're going. I'd recommend you bring a compass and perhaps even tuck a roll of surveyor tape in your shirt pocket. Use it to mark your route in and out. Several access points look deceptively easy on the way in to the water, but when it's time to turn around and go home, look-alike footpaths can leave you in a slightly confused state. Come to think of it, save room in your jacket or rain coat for a head lamp with fresh batteries. It could prove to be a godsend, particularly if you run into foul weather and nightfall is drawing close.

You are smarter than many of your fellow anglers, by the way, if you explore the more remote areas of Wiscoy Creek in the morning, and not after dinner.

About 13 miles of the Wiscoy flow through Wyoming County, and 9.4 miles of that total, or 72 percent, is marked "public fishing." Anglers who are fascinated by the historical aspects of their sport realize that fisheries management innovations or trends may occur on small streams as well as rolling rivers. The heritage of angling in Wiscoy Creek is not as rich, perhaps, as encountered in the Catskills region of New York, but much important ground has been broken in this fine stream.

In the 1930s, when farmers sometimes had to sell most of their land to keep the rest of it out of foreclosure, some of the survivors staved off economic collapse by selling public fishing rights to the state. Later, the Civilian Conservation Corps (CCC) pioneered log-, stone- and wire stream improvement devices as a means of improving trout habitat on Wiscoy Creek. Later on, in 1972, the stream was the first in the state where state biologists tried and succeeded in pulling back a bit from standard stocking strategies. In fact, stocking was curtailed altogether on the stream, and the last time I checked (in the winter of 2016–2017), hatchery transplants had not been turned loose in Wiscoy Creek for 45 years. If the no-stocking policy hurt the fishing to any degree, I've never noticed.

NORTH BRANCH WISCOY CREEK

RATING: ★★★★ (4 stars)

BEST TIME TO FISH: Late June, when aquatic and terrestrial insects combine to keep trout looking to the surface for their supper.

BEST METHOD: Cast around shaded, overhanging limbs on a breezy afternoon. Trout will be looking for whatever falls in.

The trout which hug the weedy, gnarly-looking thicket that has grown up along the margins of the North Branch of Wiscoy Creek in Wyoming County don't have a clue that their home stream may be one of the most talked-about fisheries in the northeastern United States. Oh, these fish are smart enough to know what time of day their inner dinner bell will start ringing, and trout might notice a prickly sensation as a heron is poised to give them a sharp poke in the back, but the bottom line is, trout don't read, and they don't watch any TV fishing shows, either.

So tell me, if these trout which live in the 10- to 20-feet-wide North Branch are all so big and smart and interesting, what's the rest of the story? What sets this fishery apart from others?

For starters, the North Branch now holds more trout per acre or mile than any other stream in its county. Its headwaters are about a mile west of Smith's Corners in the town of Wethersfield. To find the beginnings of this little gem of a fishing hole, look in your trusty DeLorme road atlas for Route 78, the main drag in the hamlet of Hermitage. Take 78 west from there to the first "y" shaped intersection you come to. Bear left (south) and you will find yourself on state Route 362. The North Branch can be seen from there on your left. Stay on that road all the way to Bliss, where the North Branch joins the main stem of Wiscoy Creek. It's only a three-mile run, but every inch is a joy to behold, for reasons which follow:

- In recent years, wind farms have sprouted from the North Branch's surrounding landscape, and the startling sight of those huge whirling windmills gave me a vague sense of foreboding until I remembered the film versions of H.G. Wells' sci-fi masterpiece, *War of the Worlds*. The Martian war machines in the movies looked a lot like giant, walking wind mills, and they wreaked horror on the pitiful earthmen with some kind of ray gun disintegrators, did they not? If you haven't seen the movies, one of which starred Gene Barry and the other a star vehicle for Tom Cruise, you haven't missed very much. You will definitely want to get a good look at all those Wyoming County windmills, however.

- Access to Wiscoy Creek is easy at some marked fisherman "walk-in" areas between Bliss and Pike, but less than a third of the North Branch is open to the fishing public.

- This is exclusively a trout fishery, and virtually all-wild, to boot. The North Branch was once noted for its beautiful brook trout, but, starting in the '50s, state biologists believe, browns took over the place, as they have been known to do elsewhere. Meanwhile, the North Branch hasn't been stocked with trout of any kind for at more than half a century.

- Ray Kegler, who owns about 450 feet of the North Branch but does not allow public fishing, had extensive habitat-improvement work done there a few years ago. The work had dramatic effect, as the property wound up with more and deeper pools, colder water temperatures and denser shade. When it was finished, the trout density at Kegler's place was estimated, depending on the year surveys took place, at between 3,450 and 6,475 adult wild browns per mile.

Meanwhile, trout abundance in the public fishing areas above Bliss was calculated to consist of 237 browns per mile in 2006 and 1,015 in 2009. The regional DEC trout team responded by obtaining an agreement that allowed them to undertake a habitat-improvement project within hailing distance of the private water.

Funding from the Great Lakes Basin Fish Habitat Partnership was obtained for the North Branch improvements in 2010, and the actual labor began the following year. Members of the Western New York Chapter of Trout Unlimited came through with 325 volunteer work-hours during the 2011 construction phase. Observers quickly noticed that this was not your Mom's favorite trout hotel. Instead of building old-style log cribbing structures throughout the study sites, the DEC team emphasized the use of 57 "Lunker Bunkers." These structures combine lengths of wood and rocks which can be pushed into place along stream banks to provide shelter and hide fish. Properly installed, these fish hotels maximize trout densities and sometimes last for decades before repair work has to be done. Currents pick up speed and gnaw away at streambanks, making for deeper, narrower pools.

An estimated 34 percent of the 2,100 feet of stream bank included in the work-site maps was specifically used to plan and build new hide-outs for fish that needed the space. That was part of an ongoing, up-to-your-elbows-in dirt sort of research project which may require the DEC's attention for several more years, at least. The tool box assembled for the job will continue to hold a boatload of electrofishing gear as well as chest waders in a variety of sizes. How efficiently the study proceeds will depend on the availability of funding and other factors. Yet, the preliminary results look promising. Among other advances, the habitat improvements centered around the Lunker Bunkers resulted in increased numbers of 10-, 12- and 14-inch-plus trout in the project areas.

Ultimately it may be years before we know how much state crews can increase trout populations and enhance stream habitat in the North Branch, but the early results are promising. Wild trout clearly have the makings of a happy home in the public fishing areas upstream from Bliss, with trout densities exceeding 1,809 yearling or older browns per mile in one section, but there is more to stream betterment than merely encouraging big, old trout to make lots of little, young trout during the fall spawning run.

For instance, heavy predation by herons or other natural enemies could deplete a whole year-class of trout in a small stream. Storms and runoff could scour gravel from creek bottoms, temporarily leaving spawners in the lurch—lots to do, but no place to do it. Many other scenarios could be just as damaging to short-term reproductive prospects.

The bottom line is, anglers and biologists may just have to wait a while longer before they can discern a working hypothesis about the future of the North Branch of Wiscoy Creek. During the interim, there's nothing wrong with conducting your own experiments on this exciting stream.

TROUT BROOK

RATING: ★★★ (3 stars)

BEST TIME TO FISH: Late April, before the vegetation along this rugged little stream is too tough to traverse.

BEST METHOD: Worm-dunkers and bait-flippers have an edge

By now, you may have noticed that traveling on Route 39 always seems to take you to a good trout stream, no matter which way you're headed.

For example, if you head out on the highway near Fredonia, and go east to Gowanda, you're undertaking a steelhead trip to Springville. Am I right? Of course, if you keep going east and past the Scoby Dam, you've missed your chance at steelhead, for the time being. Just keep going east if that's so; for you're only a few miles from Sardinia, where Hosmer Brook flows. Beyond there, Route 39 will take you to Arcade, where Clear Creek is one of western New York's finest. And finally, here's where you might have been headed all along. I'm referring to the main stem of Wiscoy Creek and its tributaries, of course.

We covered the North Branch just a few minutes back, and the upper reaches of the Wiscoy's main channel before that. Next up is Trout Brook, which happens to hold quite a few brook trout—plus some very lovely brown trout.

As you left Arcade, your Tom-Tom or Garmin or other travel map applications should indicate you are about 11 or 12 miles short of the village of Bliss, where a no-kill section adds considerably to the allure of Wiscoy Creek. After you try the creek and its thick patches of alders and pasture grasses, reel in and drive another 4 miles to the junction hole that mixes flows of the Wiscoy with one of its most interesting feeders, namely Trout Brook, at the intersection known as "The Pike Five Corners." Just before you reach the confluence, you should see a motorists' rest area on your right, followed almost immediately by a highly visible sign that reads, simply, "Trout Brook." If you fish it more than a couple of times, you may have one of those love-hate relationships to deal with.

Do you love the evening rises at the junction hole or do you instead hate slogging your way upstream along the brook? Looking at an eight-inch brook trout pulled from the tributary, do you love it, or would you rather tie into one of the 14- to 18-inch browns that DEC electrofishing surveyors have collected in their early-autumn field investigations?

You see, Trout Brook is not all it's cracked up to be. Some days it's even better than that. To get a complete picture, you will have to stretch your legs a little, and somehow fight your way in and out of this jungle.

Did I somehow forget to mention that this stream, which flows about 3 miles from north to south before gliding into the junction hole, is closely shadowed by Hardy's Road on its way? Well, before my amnesia worsens, I should tell all that the 2012 Trout Brook study revealed the Hardy's section was populated, per mile, by an average of approximately 700 adult, wild brookies and an average of about 1,500 adult, wild browns?

Oops. And please, pardon me.

EAST KOY CREEK

RATING: ★★★ (3 stars)
BEST TIMES TO FISH: Tan and olive caddis hatch profusely from early May through June on this stream.
BEST METHODS: Put a size 14 or 16 caddis pupal imitation on your tippet, peel about 10 or 12 feet of line from your reel and cast down and across so the fly swings in front of feeding trout.

It has a reputation among Region 9 anglers for producing lots of big, hold-over browns, but perhaps East Koy Creek hasn't been its old self, lately.

From a 2011 to 2013 study, DEC fisheries experts collected data which paints a picture of a once-popular stream that now is lightly fished, for reasons as yet unknown. After peeking at the results of 1,457 angler interviews conducted by one of the DEC's seasonal technicians, the state had some surprising statistics in hand:

- The combined angler effort on the creek, for all three years, totaled 25,926 hours.

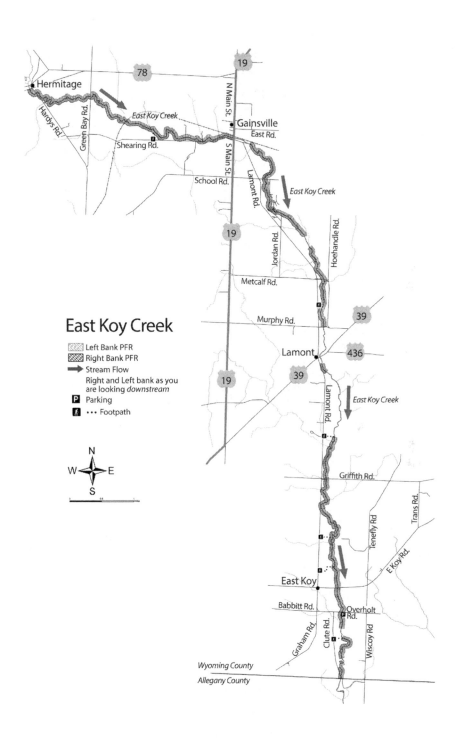

East Koy Creek

- ▨ Left Bank PFR
- ▨ Right Bank PFR
- ➜ Stream Flow
  Right and Left bank as you
  are looking *downstream*
- 🅿 Parking
- 🚶 ••• Footpath

N
W ✦ E
S

78
19
Hermitage
Hardys Rd.
Green Bay Rd.
East Koy Creek
Shearing Rd.
N Main St.
Gainsville
East Rd.
S Main St.
School Rd.
Lamont Rd.
East Koy Creek
Hoehandle Rd.
19
Jordan Rd.
Metcalf Rd.
Murphy Rd.
39
19
Lamont
436
39
Lamont Rd.
East Koy Creek
Griffith Rd.
Tenefly Rd.
Trans Rd.
E Koy Rd.
East Koy
Babbitt Rd.
Overholt Rd.
Graham Rd.
Clute Rd.
Wiscoy Rd.
Wyoming County
Allegany County

- More of that effort was logged in April than in any other month during the study. April 1, the opening day of the state's general trout season, accounted for an average of 20 percent of total angling effort during the three-year time frame.

In terms of total annual fishing effort, April is by far the busiest month of the season on the East Koy. In one of the three years studied, 76 percent of total angler effort for the year was spent in April.

There was also an electrofishing component to the study, as biologists took a close look at numbers of stocked, holdover and wild brown trout during a statewide evaluation of the DEC's fish-propagation and trout-stocking efforts. New York's DEC electrofishing "shock troops" were stunned to realize that the numbers of stocked browns remaining in the stream declined steeply between April and May, and were virtually absent from the creek by August. Yet the population of wild trout in the East Koy was fairly stable even as the stockers were doing their disappearing trick.

In five sampling studies conducted in 1996–97 and again from 2011 through 2013, the East Koy work crews collected wild fish at rates as low as 251 per mile in 1997 to as high as 494 per mile in 2011.

East Koy Creek may be one of those streams which doesn't fish quite as well as it looks. It's a moderate-size trout stream, about 15- to 30-feet wide in most spots between Hermitage and Lamont in eastern Wyoming County, but widens to about 40 feet across at Gainesville. On the bright side, it appears that wild trout numbers have held fairly steady in the last 20 years or so.

Back in the late 1990s and the 2000s, the East Koy had a reputation for growing large brown trout, but these days the heavy pull on your rod may be the work of a wild one. Electrofishing crews attest that DEC workers examine one or two trout in the 18- to 20-inch range more often than not when they are doing some electrofishing for research purposes.

The aspects of the creek that appeal the most to me are its abundant fishing rights and its varied overhead and streambank cover. These sorts of things are strong indications of a fisherman-friendly atmosphere, which means few problems with barking dogs, ample roadside pull-offs which can be used when parking areas are full, and few if any "no trespassing" warnings hung directly above state PFR signs. Most of these situations involve actions of dubious legality, and if you are worried about having any run-ins on the stream, don't be afraid to contact your regional conservation police office to ask for a clarification.

The legal access along the East Koy is very good, overall, with close to 13 miles of clearly visible yellow and green state signs starting in Hermitage and ending at the Allegany county line.

Based on fish numbers, growth rates and other data tallied during post-2000 electrofishing studies, DEC analysts often touted East Koy Creek as better than the Wiscoy for anyone who was looking for something in the range of 18 inches and up. By the time they finished any of their Wyoming County expeditions, the battery-powered water-walkers usually had statistical information to back up those opinions, too.

East Koy Creek long ago earned a reputation as a fly-fishing Mecca, and it still is known for its consistent hatches and rising trout. The seasonal progression of bugs begins with Blue Quills and little Blue winged Olives in mid-April, Hendrickson mayflies in early May and the fabled Green drakes, which are notably abundant around June 1. When these mayflies have wrapped up, teeny-weeny tricos, which are so small most men over 40 can hardly see them on cloudy mornings, start their daily mating swarms. Caddis, meanwhile, are flitting around more often than not. It's a good time to be on the fat end of a fly rod, especially on a stream like the East Koy.

To access East Koy Creek and understand where it flows in relation to other streams in DEC Region 9, note the location of Batavia, which straddles the state Thruway west of LeRoy. Take Route 98 south from Batavia to Attica. From there, turn onto Route 238 to Hermitage, where a well-hidden meadow creek begins to transform into a significant trout stream. From the spot where the creek slips under Route 20A at Halls Corner, fishing access areas are heavily used and much appreciated by anglers with miles to cover before the evening hatches. Parking areas for East Koy fans are near stream crossings at Hermitage, Gainesville, Shearing Road, Lamont, East Koy and lesser-known links between man and trout, and all have well-trampled foot paths close to the water. You can find each one with little difficulty, once you have crossed the intersection at Halls Corner (Route 20A and Route 238) and taken the next 7 miles to Hermitage. From there on, most of the better water is visible from local roads.

CLEAR CREEK (ARCADE)

RATING: ★★★ (3 stars)

BEST TIMES TO FISH: After a summer shower refreshes fish and fisherman.

BEST METHODS: Grab a 6- or 7-weight fly rod and reel, then work the pools upstream from Arcade with a flashy streamer pattern.

If you think it is hard to handicap the horses, try predicting the odds of catching a three-pound brown trout a day or two from now, in a stream bend that you fished yesterday but which might be washed off the map tonight. That's not entirely unlike fishing any day during the season in the Wyoming County section of Clear Creek.

The creek has its headwaters in Allegany County but wanders about 7 miles before linking with Cattaraugus Creek just upstream from Arcade in Wyoming County.

About 2 miles of Clear Creek are in Wyoming County, and that section is subject to erosion after every significant high-water event, but does not stay off-color for long. The lowest part, about ¾ of a mile from the junction up, has only fair fishing, at best, but the next mile and a half or so is apt to yield a fine catch to anglers willing to probe here and cast there with big, feathery streamers. Many rainbows in the six- to 10-inch mold are caught here, but brown trout of 16- to 19 inchers will slam those lively streamers, such as Black Ghosts, or Muddler minnows tied with a bit of color to show up in the muddy water, will work well.

Keep in mind that this fishery used to be considered one of the best in the Cattaraugus Creek watershed. However, populations of both browns and 'bows have been trending down lately, according to a DEC study in 2014. That one estimated the section of the river which was just tallied held approximately 282 adult wild browns and 608 wild rainbows per mile. The numbers had been a heap higher in 2007, when the calculated population was 586 wild adult browns and 1,247 rainbows per mile.

CATTARAUGUS CREEK (WYOMING COUNTY SECTION)

RATING: ★★★ (3 stars)

BEST TIME TO FISH: See recommendations for Catt's next-door neighbor, above.

BEST METHODS: The same streamers that work on Clear Creek will do fine when you try them on the Catt, but garden worms are deadly in the water just upstream from the mouth of Clear Creek.

The thing many visiting anglers love about the Arcade area is the opportunity to try something different. That "give it a try" attitude is the natural result of a meandering flood plain, but is also encouraged by the availability of 8½ miles of Public Fishing Rights and the fact that the creek is paralleled by Route 39 and Route 98 from the Erie County line to Genesee Road. Upstream from that intersection, crossroad bridges and angler footpaths off East Arcade Road.

Wild browns are regularly caught in this upper section of the Catt. So are stocked trout, with the state hatchery system supplying 5,400 yearlings and 1,000 two-year-old browns annually in the 11-mile length of the creek within Wyoming County.

MORE WYOMING COUNTY TROUT WATERS

Among other, less-known streams in the county, one that stands out is **Oatka Creek**. That's the same one that melds its currents with the pulsing springs at the state hatchery in Caledonia, but it has scant resemblance to its significant other creek. I think of it as two cold-water trout streams sandwiched around a warm-water stream—and that's exactly what's going on here.

Oatka Creek is born above the village of Warsaw. It's about 20 feet wide in spots, and it holds a mix of wild and stocked trout. Each April, the stream is re-filled with an allocation of about 1,700 yearling brookies. In May, the hatchery tanker returns with a load of about 900 yearling browns. All of the stocking takes place from Warsaw to Rock Glen. Both villages are located along Route 19, which parallels the stream.

Wild browns are also present in the upper Oatka, at least a couple of miles above Rock Glen. For some reason, the locals routinely refer to this stretch as "Cotton Creek." There are no official Public Fishing-marked locations on upper Oatka Creek, but the DEC doesn't observe many "posted" signs along this part of the stream, either. A good way to explore this stretch is to walk or drive your way from Warsaw upstream to the Glen. Your first impression might be negative, but start fishing at Mungers Road, which crosses a deep pool, and then check off all the rest, one by one.

A couple of over-looked spring creeks, **Flynn Brook** and **Pearl Creek**, might require your attention when you're in their Wyoming County neighborhoods. Flynn Brook is also known as Spring Brook, but as western New York has several of the latter, let us refer, from now on, to Flynn Brook. Located along Sullivan and Allen roads southeast of Arcade, Flynn Brook averages about 10 feet across and has a gravel bottom, besides. The most intriguing part of this stream is its mixed population of trout—browns, rainbows and brookie—that are all wild. We don't see that kind of diversity very often.

Flynn Brook is about 6 or 7 miles long, and the state was wise enough, in the dim and distant past, to acquire approximately ¾ miles of public fishing rights on the best part of the stream, which is almost due-south of East Arcade.

Compared to Flynn Brook, Pearl Creek is like Cinderella's poorest stepsister. It is posted against trespassing in a few places, and lacks any offsetting public fishing signs. Further, it is even smaller than Flynn Brook and tends to get very low and clear in the summer. Even so, it has a decent population of wild browns. It wouldn't hurt to knock on the farmer's door if you happen to be trying other waters in the area. This one is not worth a special visit, however.

PART II

SPEAKING OF TROUT

CHAPTER SEVEN

Wild Trout vs. Hatchery Trout

During my more than half a century of trout fishing I have met many anglers who assured me they were satisfied with fishing primarily for hatchery-born trout stocked in nearby streams. On the other hand, I have also conversed with anglers, mostly youngsters in their 20s, who argued adamantly about the alleged virtues of targeting wild trout, only.

Which side has got it right, these days? I'd have to say both camps are a little too tense for my tastes. First, because they waste precious fishing time snapping and snarling at each other like packs of pit bulls, and second, I know from my own experience that a lot of modern anglers, and probably the vast majority of them, can't tell a wild trout from a stocker, anyway.

I realize that's a bold declaration, and I don't mean to hurt anyone's feelings. Yet, as one who made a decent living well into my retirement years by writing and selling thousands of magazine and newspaper articles and (so far) a quartet of books on related subjects, I have broached this subject at length with state-trained and -paid aquatic biologists. I have also watched curiously as electrofishing crews sampled trout populations in dozens of brooks, creeks and rivers. Spectators were fairly common at some of these scientific outings, and friendly question-and-answer sessions were encouraged.

Sadly, most tag-alongs did not pay much attention to what the supervisors of such state-organized and financed stream surveys had to say. When I encountered some of these same fellows on my neighborhood trout waters, rods in hand, they usually had firm but mistaken opinions about the methods state research crews used to tell trout that were wild from those that weren't.

You may be muttering "as if anybody cared," or something along those lines. Yet, many dedicated anglers spend their lifetimes on the water without ever feeling compelled to tell wild trout from hatchery-reared specimens.

These fisher-folk, as a writer I admire sometimes calls them, ought to take a few moments for a closer look at the trout they hook, play and net during the current or subsequent seasons. The pay-off for so doing will be more hook-ups and landings in the near future. Depending on how often they wet a line, the people who pick up this book, focus on this chapter and put its themes and suggestions to immediate use, stand to catch several hundred more trout, wild or domesticated, over the course of a long angling career.

Before we split for another evening hatch or settle into a favorite chair with a tall, cold beer in one hand and a big-screen TV remote in the other, I should tell you the correct way to separate wild trout from those reared in concrete ponds. Then, after sharing that foamy brew, we can ditch the remote and head for a favorite trout stream without further excuses.

Your typical trout-fisher sorts his catch mentally into "wild" and "domestic" piles, then looks at each specimen's random spots and pretty colors. He should be looking at the shape of each fish's dorsal and pectoral fins. If those fins are rounded, stubby, split, torn or mangled in any other way, such injuries are rightly presumed the result of banging and scraping against the rough concrete walls commonly found in fish hatchery holding tanks. The wild trout's fins, in contrast, are flawless. Dorsal rays are straight, not bent or broken; and "pecs" are like little arrows, each one coming to a sharp point.

There you have it. Essentially, the fin inspection I've just described is the method which all modern, up-to-date experts rely upon to determine whether the trout in your hand or net is wild or hatchery-reared. It's not quite 100 percent accurate, but comes very close.

The fact that individual trout, wild or not, are very pretty to look at, means nothing if your aim is to make a positive identification with regard to the origins of the fish you catch. Pick out the most beauti-fully spotted and brilliantly colored ones you catch, in-season or while volunteering with your regional DEC electrofishing crew. After a few minutes of practice, you will have no problem at all identifying which of those trout have neatly tapered, sharply pointed pectorals and dorsal fins. Those fish are wild, regardless of whether they would win the local trout beauty contest.

The opposite is also true, i.e., any trout you catch that happens to have bent or torn fins has a hatchery pedigree. When a state electro-fishing crew scoops it out of a deep pool or riffle and plunks it down length-wise on a measuring board, the team leader will make a snap judgement, with full confidence in what he's doing. He will declare, "wild fish," or "probably stocked last spring," or, where such fish are present, might declare that the beast he holds aloft for the throngs to admire is "most likely a holdover" which was stocked one or more years before this particular survey took place. Streams with plenty of holdover trout in the general population, incidentally, provide excellent fishing, even if they are compared to other waters stuffed with wild trout.

A pretty brook trout, about 8 inches long, posed for this picture before its release into a remote western New York brook.

It wearies me to know very few anglers can consistently distinguish wild trout from those bred and fed in a hatchery environment.

I hope nobody thinks of me as being contemptuous here, for people have many motives for getting into trout fishing, and the advancement of science is way down the list. No fishermen I know of took the sport to heart for intellectual gain, although I have run into a couple who obviously were smarter than the average bear—or me, now that I think about it. Relaxation and recreation are the main goals of many who found their way into the game. Getting a few fish for the fridge now and then is a less complex and more easily satisfied motive, and if we anglers wished to organize one of those annoying television focus groups, we could come up with many more plausible explanations as to why we do what we do.

But even if he is fishing just for the heck of it, the angler who can't distinguish wild trout from the pen-reared kind is short-changing himself. If the browns, brookies and rainbows in your watershed are all eating like pigs, the usual reason is a heavy runoff after a rain storm or a very dense emergence of aquatic insects. Fishermen are not treated to such a wild-eyed feeding frenzy very often. When food, fish and angler are all in the right place, at the right time, a serious trout fanatic has a shot at hooking and landing more than a dozen or even two dozen trout in an hour or two. In most circles, such catch rates are a badge of success. They are solid proof that the angler in question has brought his "A-Game" to the stream bank, and knows how to use it.

So, what's it going to be? Will you admire the pretty black and red spots along the yellow or butterscotch flanks of the brown trout you catch this day, and assume these fish are wild? Or can you do a better job of fish I.D. today and every day hereafter, by focusing on the dorsal and pectoral fins and declaring these clues to be sure-fire indicators that most of your hook-ups are between you and wild trout?

Once you have the knack for it—and that shouldn't take more than a couple of hours of hanging out with a state electrofishing crew in August or September—you can use this seemingly trivial bit of information to catch more trout, most of the time, no matter where you do your fishing.

This brown trout is undoubtedly a wild brown. Although the dorsal fin isn't visible in this photo, the sharp pectoral fins are. That's a dead-giveaway of a wild trout in most places.

This less brilliantly colored brown is just as surely a hatchery fish, with a very gnarly dorsal fin, plus stubby pectoral fins.

Now, I appreciate the determination of many anglers to play hooked trout as quickly as possible and release all or most of a day's catch without harm. Yet it behooves fishermen to take at least a quick look at every trout they land—especially when fishing an unfamiliar stream. Taking a few seconds to check the condition of the dorsal and pectoral fins of each trout, as mentioned a short while back, should result in a positive identification, fish by fish.

There are a couple of compelling reasons for readers to eyeball each trout they catch until they have the identification drill down pat. First of all, stocked trout and wild trout tend to behave quite differently from one and other. For example, when an angler notices trout are constantly chasing a Grey Ghost but seem unable to catch up with that venerable streamer fly pattern (or any other baitfish imitation), he is probably observing hatchery trout in action.

Trout abruptly netted from their hatchery trenches and ponds for an April stocking run are used to having great gobs of food pellets hurled in their direction, in the same place and at the same time, daily. They usually get enough to eat, but they have also endured empty stomachs at times because the seasonal technician charged with keeping all the fish in the hatchery fat and happy occasionally misreads the recommended feeding rates on a bag of chow. That, or he might spend too much time trying to impress that girl who worked at the local agricultural feed emporium.

I am not disparaging any hatchery technician, real or apocryphal, for it is honest work, and so long as it is done properly most of the time, the annual crop of fish in the hatchery should turn out just fine. Meanwhile, the angler who drops in for a pre-season visit and checks his watch at the appropriate time knows the hour when dinner is served at the hatchery. After the residents have been stocked in area streams, they will likely be feeling very hungry at the same hour that he and his relatives used to be fed at the hatchery. That information, alone, can be put to good use for days or weeks after the stocking tankers have made their annual trips.

Trout stocked near the hatchery may need a few days to find some dependable places to feed in the wild. Until the food search becomes a mission accomplished, quelling their hunger will completely occupy their time. That desperate goal explains a lot of odd behavior, including the previously described mad dash after Grey Ghost streamers and other meaty-looking minnow imitations, such as a black Wooly Bugger or the ever-popular Black-nosed Dace bucktail. The newly introduced trout were not especially stupid, nor were they even unusually slow.

But do you know that old saying, "timing is everything?" Well, apparently it's true, and those stocked trout with which I was playing were way off their usual mark. Despite having out-swam thousands of their brothers and sisters to sinking scoopfuls of tasty trout pellets, they were suddenly too fast, too slow, too clumsy or too something else to chase down natural foods. My addition of an attention-grabbing wet fly to the bend of a streamer hook merely helped some rather inexperienced fish to zero in on targets that were a little different than the food items they had previously depended upon.

I have been confronted with this situation a few times, most recently in the upper Genesee River. Invariably, the stocked trout would wear themselves out, and I would elect to slow my retrieve in order to give the fish a bit more time to catch up with my streamer. In most cases, this slight adjustment simply caused the hatchery fish to be a little more cautious. Since "slower" didn't work all that well, I elected to go with "smaller" for a bit. For example, I frequently replaced a size 6 Grey Ghost with a less intimidating size 10.

Eventually, I would start to wonder if these fish might be fooled if I added an attractor of some sort to my rig. I clipped a 10- or 12-inch length from a tippet spool in my fly vest and tied one end of it to the bend of the streamer fly hook. Next, I selected a size 12 Royal Coachman wet fly, or perhaps the Queen of Waters in the same size. Either way, the aim was to select a fly that would be easily seen in the clear or slightly murky water I happened to be fishing, yet had lots of built-in action, courtesy of some spiraled brown hackle or else that wiggled in the moderate current flows.

Since I began to use it during the 1990s, the tandem rig had not deceived many wild trout, but stocked rookie trout must have linked it, somehow, to the tasty pellets they had lived on during the good old days at the hatchery. The fishing with this two-fly set-up was almost always good, but it was at its very best when my time on stocked water coincided with the usual time to come and get it at the fish factory.

Wild trout are used to feeding on a schedule, of sorts, but their dining routines typically aren't all-day, year-round affairs. The Hendrickson mayflies that hatch on the upper Genesee near Shongo, for instance, generally start popping in late April, with the most predictable rises occurring at 2 or 3 o'clock in the afternoon. Other insects, such as the tiny Trico mayflies on East Koy Creek near Gainesville, show up at 8 or 9 a.m. from early July into September.

Yet another template for fly fishers is the famous Green Drake mayfly hatch on Wiscoy Creek, which spreads its mating and egg-laying over a period of one to two weeks, often peaking just after Memorial Day. The insects hatch sporadically at all hours of the day, except that molting spinners don't appear until just before dark. As virtually all trout in Wiscoy and its North Branch, as well, are stream-born, they are seldom gullible, and any fisherman will need clever imitations and should also able to deliver accurate casts and drag-free floats if he or she hopes to have many hook-ups during the drake emergence.

Connecting with wild food sources after a couple of years of easy living in the hatchery system, as stockers eventually must do, is more difficult than one might think. The task is especially frustrating in streams which are running high and muddy after recent downpours, but fish stocked during low-water periods also have a hard time adjusting to their new surroundings. In western New York, long sections of creek channels are apt to go bone-dry during actual droughts. Trout cope with the stressful conditions by migrating into areas which have numerous spring seeps or abandoning shriveled pools in search of cooler temperatures and more varied food sources.

These fish are so adaptive that they instinctively turn away from areas which, just a few weeks earlier, offered an abundance of both food and cold currents. Now in need of regular meals as well as lower water temperatures, trout temporarily abandon their habit of selectively dining on certain aquatic insects and become "opportunistic feeders," instead. That is a complimentary way of saying that when times are difficult, trout have no compunctions against eating whatever happens to be on the menu.

In many waters which hold stocked trout, the fish "school" immediately upon their release from hatchery tankers. If a day-long pulse of rain water, intense fishing pressure or some other circumstance gives them a nudge, stockers may start to spread out from roadside pools and other likely release points. However, stocked trout often school up again in mid-or late summer, when they are spurred into movement by receding water levels and other factors that might impinge on their survival.

You probably have noticed, as well, that stocked trout sometimes form late-season schools in tributaries or spring-fed creeks which have adequately cold temperatures but sometimes run short on the kind of overhead cover—branches and the like—that would help them hide from otters, water snakes, herons and other predators. If these stockers have not yet acquired the chase-and-capture skills which seem to come naturally to wild fish, the formation of schools may attract numerous avian enemies and thereby result in higher than normal casualty rates. Then again, if the low-water situation is sufficiently dire, the schooling instinct could help larger trout, wild or domesticated, that manage to stay on guard and huddle at the head of the chow line until the crisis comes to a halt for a spell.

In any case, schooling is a last-ditch tactic for trout in most streams, and in a typical year, it is a short-term event. The group behavior can end abruptly after one or two post-Labor Day showers. Anglers can expect a predictable drop in water temperatures as days grow shorter, yet the streambank foliage lingers long enough to provide plenty of shade to cool off the shallows. Spawning time is drawing near for both brown and brook trout, too. With all of this going on, it is more than a simple coincidence that late August and September frequently are marked by some of the year's best trout fishing.

Here are a couple of other observations about hatchery trout and their wild cousins that might be good for a few extra fish this season.

RESPONSE TO PREDATORS. Perhaps the most noteworthy difference between wild and hatchery-born trout is their reaction to predators. Wild trout are aware of the threats posed by birds of prey, aquatic fur-bearers and other natural enemies almost as soon as they are born. Because of that in-bred wariness, they are more likely than hatchery trout to live through the next attack, whether the enemy comes from high overhead (osprey), a near-shore ambush (mink), or the shadows beneath an overhanging bush (northern water snake). It seems very unlikely that any trout raised for stocking purposes is smart enough to know what's coming after them once they have been dip-netted into a hatchery truck and turned loose in a nearby river or creek.

Yet some predation is in store for trout, wild or stocked, in most New York streams. The angler who has not startled a heron or two while driving or hiking between fishing spots needs to get out more and keep his eyes open, while he's at it. Herons aren't the only sights he's not seeing!

Although hatchery personnel are sometimes reluctant to discuss the situation, it is plain fact that federal, state and local fish-production facilities all have heron problems to worry about. The body counts in some New York hatcheries are deeply discouraging. Carpenter's Brook hatchery, funded by Onondaga County taxpayers to make sure Syracuse-area anglers meet the state's stocking quota in streams like Nine Mile, Butternut and Limestone creeks, loses up to 1,000 trout annually to herons. The birds have few problems wriggling into or under plastic mesh covers which were designed for the specific purpose of keeping them out.

TO CREEL, OR NOT TO CREEL

New York state in general, and especially the six counties (Erie, Niagara, Wyoming, Chatauqua, Allegany and Cattaraugus) which comprise the DEC's Region 9 administrative unit, give trout fishermen ample opportunities to live by their own ethical codes.

Do you like to keep a few for the pan, occasionally? In recent years, western New York anglers have been permitted to creel up to five trout a day, with the stipulation that only two of the five could be longer than 12 inches during the statewide trout season from April 1 through October 15. At the other end of the sporting spectrum, many streams now remain open for catch and release angling from Oct. 16 through March 31, from the end of one season to the start of the next.

Some anglers actually complain about this situation (punctuating their feelings with derisive descriptions of "Philadephia lawyers"), but I am loathe to turn down any extra fishing time put forth by the DEC.

The real quandary facing anglers when regulations are unusually generous is whether it is wise to keep more trout and, if so, what precautions can be taken to assure the fish will stay fresh until dinner is served.

One of my frequent fishing pals, retired police officer John "Kid" Corbett, tucks a cooler and a bag of ice in his car when his wife requests a couple of trout for dinner. If he's fishing the shoreline of a lake, he puts his fish on a stringer until quitting time. The routine is quite different when he's wade-fishing a trout stream. Instead of carrying a stringer slung from his hip, Corbett quickly kills his catch by breaking its neck or giving it a whack with a thick branch. On warm days, especially those when he does not wish to hurry back to his car in order to put each trout on ice, he guts the fish immediately. From that point until he is done fishing for the day, Corbett dips his creel periodically to keep his catch cool by evaporation.

No-kill fishing can be extremely enjoyable at any time of year, and the DEC has firmly supported the concept in many of the better cold-water streams in Region 9. The fishing holes available to catch-and-release anglers as of early 2017 include sections of more than 15 streams. However, because these special regulations are subject to change as frequently as every other year under current state policies, sportsmen enroute to unfamiliar waters are advised to double-check any rules of which they are not absolutely certain.

Catch and release angling strictures are a great test of angling skills, whether they are in force during regular seasons or—more typically in New York state—are applied from the end of one season on Oct. 16 until the start of the next on March 31. Trout that are of better-than-average size are present in such spots, and fishermen who give them a go have a decent chance of hooking a personal-best trout. You can be certain that the sportsmen and women who haunt stream sections bearing the "no-kill" label won't make many return trips unless they encounter Leviathan, or at least the local version of such mythical beasts, catching a few "eating fish." The dream came true for a fellow member of a western New York fishing club who twitched a streamer fly through a deep pool last December. Naturally, I was sworn to secrecy before he would give me a look at the trout's smart phone portrait.

"You couldn't eat a trout like that," this fellow said. "If I did, half of my friends would want to kill me. So when I got that one in my net, I just held it under water, and looked at it until it was fully recovered from the fight. I'm not kidding when I tell you that was a 30-inch brown."

WILD FISH ARE THE WARIEST. Although I love catching hatchery trout even after publicly funded snacking sprees and three squares a day have left them as dumb as fence posts, the warmer place in my heart is reserved for wild trout. The two-year-old brown trout that DEC crews currently stock in some of the better and more loved and protected streams throughout the state are mostly 13 to 15 inches long, and pretty darned good-looking, too. However, the primary reason they are so popular is that they get more food and an extra year to grow, as well. The drab, pale-tan browns that are stocked in the spring of the year stretch out, in most waters, to a maximum length of 8 or 9 inches, which is barely half as long as the two-year-olds raised at state hatcheries. Unfortunately, from the perspective of both fisheries managers and serious anglers, the two-year-olds don't gain any wisdom or wariness from being stocked a year late.

When the DEC began stocking large numbers of two-year-old browns, and soon after that adopted regulations which prohibited individual sportsmen from keeping more than two trout longer than 12 inches, the announced rationale was to spread the wealth among more anglers. Before then, it was possible for one fishing license holder to creel five trout a day, plus, in some counties, five additional brook trout of 8 inches or better. During that period, anglers who lived close to a heavily stocked creek or had work days off in the middle of the week found they had a huge advantage over fishermen who couldn't get in on the fun until Friday or Saturday.

Once the so-called "Five and Two Rule" was adopted—limiting anglers in most streams to keeping a maximum of five trout a day, and only two of those being longer than a foot—it came as a shock to many of us just how easy it was to catch a brace of 12-inch hatchery browns. The wild trout were a different matter, of course. They were not impossible to catch, but anglers fairly proficient with flies, lures or live bait frequently found themselves doing a creel check at the end of the day and not finding a single wild trout in a basket that was otherwise stuffed with four or five stockers.

Some of the highest quality trout fishing available in DEC Region 9 in recent times was found in streams like Wiscoy Creek, which hasn't been stocked for decades now. Another set of regulations that has resulted in productive fishing for many western New York anglers is the split-calendar rule that has one set of regulations permitting the capture of several fish a day from April 1 through Oct. 15, but gives the go-ahead to catch-and-release fishing in the same waters from October 16 through March 31. This proviso gives anglers new opportunities to try their luck on previously unfamiliar streams throughout the balance of the year.

Incidentally, when you have determined that the stream you are fishing is top-heavy with stocked fish, you can count on finding numerous targets of opportunity close to bridges, along well-maintained creek access roads and other spots not far removed from fisherman parking areas.

These days, it's very difficult for hatchery workers to enlist sufficient numbers of volunteers to lug buckets of 7- to 9-inch yearling trout—or even the more coveted DEC two-year-old browns that usually measure between 13 and 16 inches—to remote locations. Many stocking volunteers have been doing this chore annually for many years, and are rightly proud of the effort they make each April and May. They deserve considerable credit for their hard work, which has kept a few trout fisheries from fizzling. Unfortunately, experienced trout-stockers are outnumbered in some areas of western New York by anglers who are willing to get out of bed early and then wait at hatchery gates until state trucks power up their engines and begin dumping their latest quotas of hatchery browns, brooks and rainbows into neighborhood creeks. These self-centered, greedy anglers aren't at all interested in giving hatchery crews a little help. Instead, they follow state trucks over back roads, wait until the DEC workers and volunteers dump a hefty load of trout, and then fish their way back home. Talk about fresh fish—often, truck followers have their daily limit of fish in a creel and are on their way home before the stocking crews have finished their own run.

The hatchery workers and their helpers are, in general, disgusted by the truck followers, but can do little about the situation other than to tinker with their trout-release schedules or take a wrong turn now and then.

Frequently, the creel-stuffers follow DEC crews until they have loaded a few pools with fresh fish. At that point, the sneaky types will gear-up and fish their way back toward the hatchery. The participants in this easy, sleazy cat-and-mouse game are used to coming home with limit catches, but otherwise have nothing to brag about.

In my youth, anglers who sat around near road pull-offs while waiting for the stocking truck to show up were openly scorned. The fishermen who were truly admired and appreciated in long-ago times left their rods and reels home on days when the state tankers were out and about. How sad that these conservation-minded ladies and gentlemen are in short supply now! The trout-stocking quotas put together by state fish culturists and biologists today must allow for the fact that a full bucket of trout can't be carried any farther than a pair of 70-year-old legs can hike.

CHAPTER EIGHT

Some Big Trout Live in Tiny Houses

You will never hear me speak ill of small trout or small streams, I promise. For there is no type of angling that poses more challenges or rewards than fishing in miniature. I began my angling career when I was just 3½ years old, and the quarry was whichever species happened to be hungry when Dad got home from work in time to take me fishing. Until I was 10 years old, at least, my fishing was done mainly in Stopyro's Brook, a tributary of Nine Mile Creek that is located about mid-way between the villages of Marcellus and Skaneateles in southern Onondaga County.

Nine Mile was then and remains today one of the better trout fisheries in the Syracuse area. Stopyro's, however, is an enigmatic place that is seldom fished, except in my dreams. In the nostalgic pools of my childhood, the big prizes hiding out from diligent youngsters were carp, weighing up to 10 pounds or so. White suckers up to 15 or 16 inches long were possibilities any time one gave the brook a try, and pan fish, including bluegills and pumpkinseed sunnies, rock bass, and crappies were present. The stream also harbored some bass, both large-mouths and smallmouths, although few were of legal length, which was 12 inches in most New York waters during the 1950s.

Trout, either browns or brook trout, might have been in the population mix in Stopyro's Brook, but if they were, they must have migrated into the stream in search of food at some point, and for comfort's sake probably vacated the same stretch in the summer, when water levels dropped and temperatures rose.

Nine Mile Creek was a much different story. From Marcellus Falls downstream into the village of Camillus, Nine Mile and Route 174, the road parallel to the creek, were reconstructed during the early 1960s to accommodate increasing volumes of traffic upon the completion of the Lee-Mulroy Highway, also known these days as Route 175. Gorgeous, spring-fed pools and undercut banks were obliterated. Several stone-arch bridges were replaced with flat, poured concrete floors. Bridge work of that type replaced shady crossings with deep pockets which had held many large brown trout in the preceding years.

Fortunately for me, I was about 12 or 13 years old by then and had absorbed enough of the fishing lessons my family gave me at Stopyro's Brook to feel confident about dunking a worm or two in Nine Mile Creek. For instructive purposes, Stopyro's was basically a smaller, warmer Nine Mile. The first-named stream held a few trout, stocked and wild, for at least the first two months of the annual trout season, but you had to hunt for one—hunt hard, in fact. Sometime in June, water temperatures climbed in the creek, from the outlet at Otisco Lake down to the Marcellus Falls area. Trout thrived year-round from the falls to Camillus, thanks mainly to a series of large limestone springs, which are visible along the banks of Nine Mile today, near the Marcellus sewage treatment plant. Today, these springs pump out water that registers about 50 degrees Fahrenheit—even when air temperatures are in the 90s. Upstream from the springs, Nine Mile, with mid-summer readings in the 70s, is too warm to support trout. Downstream from the springs, the creek averages in the low 60s for most of its tumbling route into Camillus and then to the creek mouth on the shore of Onondaga Lake. Sixty-two degrees Fahrenheit is verging on perfect, as far as a trout's metabolism is concerned.

Since the stream channel and a connected series of commercial fish ponds can still be seen from the highway, I find myself wondering how much Stopyro's Brook and Nine Mile Creek, as well, really did change during the road reconstruction that took place more than half a century ago.

One thing my mentors taught me right out of the starting gate was that fish in small streams often lived in tiny, overlooked "houses." The larger fish we encountered typically avoided us by slipping under shadowy overhangs, hugging the deep side of boulders in slick runs and foaming pockets, or simply filling the unoccupied space in sharp bends and sloping gravel bars. In such "holding water," as my Dad called it, a good fish could wait for the occasional appearance of a careless minnow, crayfish or night crawler. Just about all the tackle we needed to put our targeted fish on the bank could easily fit into the airy, split-willow creels anglers carried around in those days.

Dad's gear, plus a few items that were shared by our whole platoon of anglers, could fit comfortably in any sort of tin can. We traveled extremely light on the banks of Stopyro's Brook, and even more so when we were invited to tag along on Nine Mile.

Most of my father's tackle cost mere pennies—spare hooks, split shot and that kind of thing could be acquired at a local hardware store. Undoubtedly, the most important item Dad took along was bait can full of lively worms. Not just any container would do, and the Kelly family had a distinct preference for the cans which held the Prince Albert brand of tobacco. Many smokers in that post-Depression days came to know Prince Albert for the corny jokes that went along with the tobacco, free of charge. "Where's Prince Albert?" somebody would inquire. "He's in the can," someone else replied, to a chorus of guffaws.

I guess you had to be there.

The prince's wad of tobacco was packed a bit loosely but it could easily be rolled in cigarette paper or stuffed in a pipe at any time unless Grandpa Kelly already had the "fixings" in his possession. Once the can had been emptied of tobacco and re-filled with "garden hackle," our family group of anglers was well prepared for a couple of hours of recreation. The dependable lid on the can snapped tightly shut yet opened easily, and it fit comfortably in a flannel shirt pocket. Such a fine utensil generally held about 30 plump garden worms and enough crumbly soil to give the bait some moving-around space. The budding angler who had 30 worms handy when a trip on area waters got underway could reasonably expect to catch two or three fish of one breed or another before his own rumbling stomach urged him to hurry home for some of Mother's good cooking.

The bulk of our tackle was selected with an eye for economy. Dad and my grandfathers alike seldom carried manufactured rods or reels to Stopyro's. Instead, they kept sharp jack knives in their pants pockets, along with a wooden dowel that served to carry the troop's supply of fishing line. The chalk line used to lay out our back yard garden was suitable for hooking panfish and hurling them behind us when they bit. We also needed a couple of leaders which were soaked in wet felt pads so they would not turn brittle, and of course, a few medium-size sinkers and maybe a dozen Kirby-style hooks. Also, if somebody remembered to bring them along, we usually threaded a nickel-diameter piece of cork on each line. They made excellent floats, and kept our baits drifting with the currents, just off the stream bottom.

Before rigging up, the leaders of our safari had to find a couple of willow branches that were just the right length and suitably springy at the tip-end for fishing an intimate creek.

Our expeditions did not usually involve more than a few adults and kids at a time. Four or five people would be a bunch, and two or three participants were more typical. The smaller the group, the more the youngest among us could catch and the more knowledge any single angler in the making could absorb. As I was an eager student and often had Dad's undivided attention, I soaked up fishing tips in a hurry. Naturally, I didn't the get the hang of every suggestion (or order) right away, but it made me proud when I heard Dad confide to a long-time friend that "Mike is the real fisherman in the family."

Perhaps the most important lessons were those which focused on fish and the places where they live. Initially, this seemed pretty obvious. Fish lived in Stopyro's Brook, right? But as time flew by, and Dad and I spent more hours on Nine Mile Creek itself and less time on its tributaries, this instruction proved to be more difficult than I thought it would. My father, a bait fisherman who in his 50s became a very skillful nymph fisherman, had my respect always, but I wasn't the greatest listener, and it took me a long time to catch on to Nine Mile Creek and its nuances, despite my father's careful directions. When I was 10 years old—10 years and about four months, to be more precise—I was very frustrated because my bait seldom landed in the "tiny houses" where the bigger trout were reputed to live. Consequently I would lift my bait up and out of the water and flip it again—somehow, missing all of my targets, every time.

"Can't catch 'em if your worm isn't in the water," Dad declared. "Do you want me to hook one, so you'll know how to do it, next time?"

He must have perfected the art, that afternoon. Over and over again, he would point me toward what struck him as a good spot, but I just wasn't getting it. I supposed those tiny houses were visible to him but not to me, and I told him so. It was as if a lightbulb switch went off in his head.

"Why didn't you say so?" he said. He laughed merrily as he realized this small bump in the road was entirely his fault. He had taught me to make precise casts that would splash the bait down in a trout feeding lane, time after time. But he hadn't bothered with a warm-up cast, and as a result, he had taught me to cast in a certain direction, but hadn't mentioned anything about distance. He realized, too, that the trout houses in Dad's favorite section of Nine Mile Creek, downstream and across the road from Pete's tavern, were all a little bit beyond my casting reach.

"This would be a good time to have that soft drink," said my father. He popped the top of the root beer he had purchased from Pete and excused himself, briefly.

"I almost forgot, I have something for you," he said. "I'll be right back, just sit still for a few minutes. He walked across the road to his parked car and opened the trunk. A minute later he was walking toward me again, and carrying a cardboard tube with a screw-on top. I had an idea what he was up to, but didn't say anything.

Inside the cardboard was a three-piece Heddon bamboo fly rod, 8 feet and 10 inches long. The missing two inches were victims of a wind-blown car door but the tip had been neatly repaired. Dad reached inside his willow creel and removed a matching, single-action Pflueger fly reel, spooled with a 30-yard-long floating line. A six-foot leader completed the outfit.

"That's Grandpa Kelly's rod," I said, having used it a couple of times when the old man still enjoyed an occasional outing at Stopyro's or some other spot with easy walking. I didn't know what emphysema was, exactly. I did know it was now keeping Grandpa from his old hang-outs along Nine Mile and its tributaries.

"He thought you might like to use it, for now," Dad said. "It's been his favorite for a long time, so I want you to promise you'll take good care of it."

"I will," I replied. "I promise."

I carefully removed the rod from the tube and slid it out of the protective flannel bag that came with it. With Dad's help, I had everything ready to go in a few minutes.

One quirky thing about those old bamboo rods was their penchant for picking up tiny pieces of grit that might slide into the female ferrule. At my request, Dad showed me how to lubricate the male ferrule with the skin oil on my nose, and he also demonstrated the use of a swatch of steel wool to smooth out any rough patch near the connection.

"I'll take good care of it," I said.

For the next half hour or so, I fished diligently but with no success. Some days, the trout don't seem inclined to eat, no matter what you toss their way. But we had a bunch of worms in our Prince Albert tobacco cans, and the conditions that May afternoon seemed just right.

I didn't have any hip boots that season, so when Dad led me up the creek to the side channel behind the old mill, he announced he was going to carry me rock to rock through the knee-deep current. We opted to do the crossing Indian-style, my arms around his neck and his arms holding my legs over his hips. I made it, bone-dry, and Dad was happy to see that his rubber hip boots were leak-free, too.

The fishing was still slow as the sun sat momentarily on the top of the gorge, but Dad pointed to the little patch of quiet water about 10 feet downstream from where I stood.

"That's a real good spot," he said. "Here's what I want you to do. Put the bait right next to that little branch sticking up in the water. Give it a couple of casts. If you get a bite, let the fish take it before you set the hook."

I followed his instruction to the letter, and when the rod tip began to bounce, I asked Dad the critical question.

"Now?"

"Yes, now," he said. And when I set the hook, the fish tugged back, hard, but I had it flopping on the bank within 10 seconds, at most.

It was not a large fish, perhaps 9 inches or a bit longer, but my brook trout—my *first* brook trout—was so pretty that I could not take my eyes off it. I have no words to convey its beauty, but in my mind I can still see it, smell it, even taste it. After eating my special trout supper and showing my new rod to Mom and my siblings one more time, I drifted upstairs to get ready for bed. I lay awake for nearly an hour, then fell asleep. Later that night I woke up, then fell back to sleep and dreamed about my trout again.

I did not know it yet, but one of my fishing buddies told me nobody forgets his first trout. Although I can't speak for everyone, the memories of that fish and the "tiny house" where it lived are as clear now as they ever were. I would not want it to be any other way.

TAKE A KID FISHING, THE RIGHT WAY

Not all of the countless dads, grandparents, siblings and other folks who try to initiate young anglers into the rituals of trout fishing do so successfully. The path to angling proficiency has its share of stops, jumps and wrong turns. Some fishing instructors are quickly discouraged and give up the game after taking part in one or two "passing it on" sessions at local tackle shops or rod and gun club casting ponds. The problem isn't always stupid fishermen; sometimes, it's smart fish.

Ray Besecker, a friend who taught basic fishing skills to hundreds of wide-eyed youngsters as a volunteer at angling clinics sponsored by Cornell University's Sportfishing and Aquatic Resources Program, counseled fathers to focus their initial lessons on sunfish, rather than trout. Consequently, even when he was dealing with prospective trout fishers, Besecker preferred to call his classes to order on the banks of ponds, lakes and streams which were loaded with jumbo bluegills. As long as he had a few sunnies in casting range, he and his pupils could catch a few, and those small triumphs became springboards to other achievements.

Here are a few more tips for parents and others who wish to guide their kids into trout fishing, Besecker's way.

Derbies. Parents with large families and strenuous jobs sometimes see sponsored fishing derbies as a great way to get the job done in a hurry. Single moms and fathers who had little free time owing to their need to work second shifts find this notion very appealing. Unfortunately, derbies typically are annual events, and contestants may have no opportunities to work on their skills until next year's extravaganza. By the time participating children are 16 years old and required to purchase a license in order to try their luck, they have already lost interest in the sport.

Role models. Whether the duty falls to Dad, Gramps, Mom or Mom's boyfriend, beginner anglers benefit greatly from having a steady, long-term relationship with an experienced trout fisher—in other words, a mentor. Mentors do more than just show up in time for the local derby. They also are available to take the newcomer fishing several times a year, and to answer questions about trout that come out of the blue over smart phones, email or other modern means of research.

Safety. The most important concern of any rookie angler (and his parents) is safety, and that goes double for budding trout fishermen, who wade swift currents and therefore must be extra cautious. Most adult anglers use waders with felt or cleated soles, and they lean on wading staffs as if these simple sticks were third legs. Despite these safety measures, every trout fisher is going to slip and fall once in a while. Mentoring adults should stay close to their pupils, and warn them to avoid slippery rocks and other wading hazards as much as possible.

Return the favor. Experienced trout anglers who take away their own quality time by spending many hours teaching kids will be rewarded over the ensuing years. Frequently, pupils who owe a debt of gratitude to their angling mentors will repay them as the years pass, by supplying transportation to favorite fishing holes, occasionally dropping off a fish for the freezer, or even tying knots that are a challenge to aging anglers who have failing eye sight.

CHAPTER NINE

Becoming a Nymphing Ninja

The idea of letting a clipboard bang against your hip while you plunge into thickets of Japanese knotweed or multiflora rose would be more than most trout fisherman could tolerate, but competitors in the trout tournaments that are held almost every spring or summer weekend near Syracuse and Rochester are used to it. My friends and I don't like the trend, but cash-prize tourneys have become pretty popular in some parts of New York. When the competition is fierce, it's not unusual to count 20 or more cars crowded in or around angler-access spots on some of our busier trout waters, especially in July and August. I am told these events are staged mostly during the summer because the contestants do not wish to disturb other anglers who have no time off to fish, other than weekends. If so, good for them, but I still can't picture myself distributing envelopes stuffed with paper money or hoisting a trophy aloft at some awards ceremony.

The next thing you know, we trout fishers will be wearing Nascar-type shirts with sponsor names plastered all over them: Columbia, G Loomis, Orvis and others. Where would it end? Personally, I think it will end with those clip boards. Most anglers don't want to keep score for somebody else. And besides, what's all that stuff about using the *honor system*, anyway? Who ever heard of a trout fanatic stopping long enough to tally his own catch, let alone that of another registrant in a contest?

I can think of at least one positive thing that could result from "Your R.L. Winston Eastern Circuit Fly-Fishing Championship," or whatever else the sponsors choose to call it. Namely, the gung-ho (but slightly nerdy) competitors would become better and better fishermen. Since artificial nymphs are everybody's bread-and-butter flies these days, anyone who competes in fly-fishing contests will obviously have to become a better "nymphet"—maybe even a "nymphomaniac." No, that one doesn't seem right, considering the need for us fly fishers to become role models for youngsters and such.

How would it be if we referred to these determined, life-long learners "nymphing ninjas?" It works for me, anyway.

Although I am not a nymphing ninja, my outdoors-writer pedigree will net me a free pass (free lots of things, actually) to most tournaments and give me regular shots at interviewing R.L. Winston Circuit champions about how YOU can become a better nymph flinger. Of course, we outdoors writers are living proof that you don't have to know much about interviewing in order to "git 'er done," as the hosts of more than one Outdoor Network show might put it.

And how lucky you readers must be, for nymph-fishing happens to be one of those subjects in which I am fairly conversant, even though I am clearly an amateur, and not a pro. I would be pleased, therefore, to answer some questions today, instead of always asking others to do the heavy lifting.

To avoid confusion, let's label each question with a capital **Q**—which even a dry-fly purist should be able to understand—and identify each response with a bold-face, capital **A**. Here we go.

Q: Are all trout tournaments designed mainly for nymph fishermen?

A: Yes, definitely. This is so because real aquatic nymphs and larvae account for by far the greatest share of calories that the average trout consumes on a day-to-day basis. Trout will come up to the surface to feed on mayfly duns and such if they can get enough food that way, but if bugs are scarce on top, trout will go down and stay down to conserve energy.

Q: What are some of the nymphs that are popular with tournament anglers?

A: You might be surprised at how simply most tournament flies are constructed. As a general rule, contestants do most of their fishing within a few inches of the bottom, which means weighted flies are necessary or at least helpful. Many different flies can be fished effectively, but most favorite patterns have a dozen or more wraps of non-toxic tin or other substitutes for traditional lead weight. Flies likely to get an early try in cast-about-for-trout events usually will look like caddis larvae, with the weight covered by over-wraps of lacquered floss or stretchy lengths of Uni-Thread. Many of these life-like caddis imitations also have dark thoraxes ribbed with feathery wraps of ostrich herl. In general, hook sizes 10–16 are most efficient. Most contests require barbless hooks to facilitate quick releases and minimize the potential for injured trout.

Q: How do you rig up for tournaments?

A: Assuming the choice of equipment is mostly up to you, experienced tournament anglers prefer to use long rods, from 9 feet to 10 or even 11 or 12 feet long. Leaders vary in length because the European national teams that made trout tournaments popular overseas long before they began to blossom here disdain the strike indicator set-ups that are commonly used in the United States. Instead of pinching one or two split shot onto their leaders and watching the movements of a small foam bobber to signal a strike, like your average Yank will, our Euro rivals like to use a heavily weighted fly that they can feel hopping and dragging on the bottom. It's impractical to do much more than lobbing and roll-casting the prototypical weighted flies they favor.

Most of the young anglers vying in New York tournaments call the basic approach I've outlined "Czech nymphing" but every European trout fisherman has his or her little secrets where nymphs are concerned.

Q: How do I know what species of nymphs are most common in streams where I plan to enter a couple of tournaments soon?

A: That's an easy one. Scout the stream, preferably no more than a couple of weeks in advance of the contests. Turn over some rocks, to identify nymphs that are already active and likely to hatch soon. You can tell those which are close to take-off by their almost-black wing pads and the way they cluster on sunken rocks that are in the stream's shallows. Species that are emerging on a regular basis will be stuck to the fronts of cars in fisherman parking areas or struggling to get free from spider webs under bridges.

Q: Why do I break my line so often while I'm bringing in a trout?

A: You probably need to "Czech" your line once in a while. But seriously, folks, any nymph fisherman who does a good job of keeping his fly close to the bottom is going to have problems with fraying and breaking now and then. Inspect your line for damage frequently, and bring plenty of tippet material so you won't run out during the competition.

CHAPTER TEN

Trout in Transition

What is it that makes a trout stream a trout stream? And when does it cease to be so?

I suspect most fishermen would answer these questions directly. For example, I myself would say that any river, creek or brook which consistently supports a population of trout—even a small one—should qualify for inclusion in *The World Book of Trout Streams*. If there were any such volume, that is.

To deter any readers from thinking this must be one of those time-wasting academic exercises they have heard so much about, permit me to admit there is a method to this madness. I am thinking now of two fellows I know who spend much of their free time taking overnight or dawn-to-dusk excursions to streams in central and western New York.

Their primary interest is not just trout fishing, *per se*, but fishing in places where they have an excellent opportunity to find and capture large trout. Do you see the difference? It's a bit complicated, but the picture cleared up considerably for me once I realized my two friends (who are extremely cautious about revealing their pet spots, by the way) were focused on big trout, bigger trout and even bigger trout. These two 40-something anglers did their share of fly-fishing and hatch-matching when they were home or close to it, and the streams they visited were full of browns and rainbows in all sizes up to 2XL. But when the time was right for *really* big trout—say, five- to seven-pounders—they loaded up their vehicles and hit the highway in search of places few other regional anglers had ever heard of, let alone fished.

If the water looked good when they arrived, my friends would be rigging streamer flies, shallow-running stickbaits and the juiciest, liveliest nightcrawlers they could find at Wal-Mart or the practice green at a local golf course.

This dynamic duo has a regular circuit to ride, these days, because they release many if not most of the hefty browns they haul from New York waters. When a return trip seems to be in order, they have a chance of hooking a jut-jawed lunker for a second or even a third time, and this pair has dozens of photos of the "toads" they have taken over the years.

You must be getting impatient with me. If our roles were reversed, I would be listening carefully for the exact locations of at least a couple of likely lunker lairs. Well, hold on a bit, because I'm not going to name secret pools, or blindfold you and guide you to the river bank, either. But I can give you a head start on how to find and catch a trophy or two—and in some spots you probably have yet to try.

I hope you have noticed by now that my monster-chasing friends do NOT just spot a hefty trout and fish for it in the same hole, over and over, until they have nagged a nibble out of it. A canny angler can do a whole lot better than that, if he realizes big browns are inclined to search for their supper at propitious times instead of staking out bend pools or log jams and waiting for snacks to float by. These trout are on the move at night, especially when the water is rising or falling due to dramatic changes in the weather.

If you think you are ready to go prospecting for big browns, the first thing you need to do is take lots of temperature readings with your trusty stream thermometer. But don't look only for the perfect comfort temperature range of 62 to 65 degrees. Ideally, you should fill a steno notebook—or a smart phone—with temperature data for three or four trips. Data for early morning, mid-afternoon, evening and one or two hours after sunset would be wonderful. If you can't get that much information for one reason or another, settle for a couple of late spring and early summer readings to indicate what range of temperatures will occur between the warmest part of the day (mid or late afternoon) and the coolest period, between 5 and 8 a.m. Trout, and big trout most of all, should be most active as temperatures drop through the upper and lower 60s.

When this basic information is compiled for several deep holes that you think may be home to one or more dandy browns, all you have to do is give each pool some serious attention when their residents are likely to be home.

The fish you'll be seeking under these circumstances are "in transition," which means many of them will have a series of short stays in places which come close but not close enough to meeting their requirements for cold water, steady food supplies and overhead protection, among other things. When one or several big trout pick out the same spot, you stand a reasonable chance if seeing one or more of the rough necks chasing one another from their hide-outs. These little scraps have nothing to with spawning rituals, which after all won't take place until mid-October at the earliest. Instead, these startling struggles are mostly about survival. To the victor go the spoils, including first crack at minnows, crayfish and even the field mice that a big trout needs to subsist during flood or drought.

More than one species of fish will hang out in the transition zones I'm describing. I know of a very large pool in a river—and don't ask which one—which flows under an interstate highway bridge. In the spring, this big but otherwise Plain Jane pool attracts spawning walleyes and some gigantic tiger muskellunge as well as the usual hook-jawed browns.

I won't leave this discussion without first laying out a few scenarios that are likely to present lunker-lovers with some big, transitional trout. First, don't pay heed to anyone who recommends waiting for a full moon before mounting an expedition for these fish. They, themselves, will probably schedule their own outings to coincide with a dark moon. Experience tells me that big trout move about with boldness on pitch-dark nights, most likely because they don't have to rely on their eyesight, and catch up to suckers, shiners and such by simply laying in ambush until something tasty comes close enough to be eaten.

Another hopeful circumstance is a torrential rain storm. It will result in rising, slightly muddy currents and turn on the trout, day and night. Muggy evenings are better, in the summer at least, than dry but cool nights. And long flats, muddied by runoff currents, attract schools of fallfish and other soft-rayed prey species that are tempting to heavyweight browns.

If you seem to seem to be running low on king-size browns in the pools you like to fish, change locations for a trip or two. Trout in transition sometimes zig when they ought to zag, and the fishermen seeking them occasionally make the same mistake.

FIVE TIPS TO MAKE YOU A BETTER TROUT FISHERMAN

If you've already tried the following suggestions, spend some time this season reviewing your own rules about why, where and how an angler might improve his daily and seasonal trout-fishing efficiency. Any fisherman who thinks he knows all there is to know about trout and trout streams must have flipped his "on" switch sometime in the past. The following adaptations are among the most important decisions I've made during my 60-plus years wading in cold water. Many more revelations are yet to come, I hope!

1. Get up earlier and (try to) stay out longer. This is a tactic that every young angler tries at some point in his or her trout-seeking career. It works very well on the first day of the season, when the population of wild and holdover trout has been augmented by pre-season stockings of hatchery-bred fish. However, take a siesta around lunch time when you're fishing hard. If you burn both ends of the candle for too many years, months or weeks, you'll run out of light. Remember, trout fishing is supposed to be fun, not exhausting.

2. Practice knots at home, not on the water. Tying knots is increasingly difficult as an angler grows older, but struggling with old favorites like the improved clinch (tippet to fly) or double surgeon's knot (connecting leader with line) isn't any easier during strong breezes or fading sunlight.

3. Long rods are a trout fisher's secret weapon. Many anglers will insist that the opposite is true, but I am personally convinced that a fly rod of 8½ to 9½ feet in length is perfect for dry, wet, nymph or streamer fishing, and anybody who puts his faith in a

nightcrawler or any other live bait will be amazed at the fishability of an even longer stick. My pet bait rod is an 11-foot noodle rod which bends over nearly double when a big fish is on the hook. The manufacturer recommends it for use with 4- to 8-pound mono, and I seldom go higher than 4-pound test. My largest fish on the rig was a 30-pound chinook salmon.

4. To catch more and bigger trout, lighten up a little. If you use 6-pound-test monofilament for bait and lures and stubbornly stick to tippets of 5X or heavier when you're fly fishing, consider going one size lighter from here on. The most dramatic improvement I ever made with regard to terminal tackle was my decision to re-spool my bait reel (which is actually a single-action fly reel) with 4-pound line. Second in significance was my change-over from a 30-inch tippet testing at 5X to a thinner, lighter 6X tippet. Both of these changes gave me a more flexible, sensitive and drag-free connection between line and hook. Yes, I do break off a large brown or rainbow on occasion, but I hook more big boys and land more, too, since I made the switch.

5. Broken rods are absolutely unnecessary. And I should know, since I've broken more than my share. I've owned 20-some fly rods in my day, and broken four. All of these sickening separations between grip and tip were the result of my habit of not watching where I was going. As a teenager, I watched a pretty girl when I should have been watching for the patch of weeds that reached up and grabbed the tip end of my old bamboo fly rod as I rode a bicycle through a county park. A few years after that, I left a fiberglass rod on top of my car when I had tucked everything else safely inside the vehicle. Then came the day that saw me trip and fall on my hands and knees when I was sneaking along the bank of Catharine Creek. I landed smack-dab on my hands, including the one that was holding my 10-footer.

You get the idea, I'm sure. Every rod is at risk of breaking, and as more and more fly rods cost upwards of $300, we anglers pay a steep price for our carelessness.

CHAPTER ELEVEN

A Trout-Fisher's Diary

If anybody out there honestly believes most or all trout fishermen are chronic liars—well, permit me to say such cynical folks need to get educated, right now. Reputations are at stake, and besides, we're starting to see some impressive rises this time of the day, at the Campground Pool. That last disturbance looked and sounded like a U-boat depth charge, the way it left a suction hole and a ring of bubbles at the surface of Wiscoy Creek, down there in that little village in Wyoming County. What do they call that community? Oh yes, I remember now: "Bliss." It is a nice name for a fishing town.

People who scoff at some of the more outlandish quotes attributed to trout fishermen—including catch and release totals that are dubious if not mathematically impossible to achieve under normal fishing circumstances—might get a better sense of the facts if they had a chance to skim through my personal fishing diaries.

These stacks of scribblings cover all or parts of 40 New York trout seasons. From the early 1970s through my retirement from the Syracuse *Post-Standard* in March, 2007, I never grafted a single fib to those hallowed pages, nope, not even one. And why should I? The volumes were written by me and for me, although I still get a warm and fuzzy feeling, every now and then, if I get a chance to cite an anecdote from my dairy to reinforce a point made earlier in a magazine article or a book chapter.

My diaries were written one or two pages a time after each day on the water. They were never meant to serve as a brick wall of defense between writer and reader. Rather, I intended them to function as mini-encyclopedia, which were researched, composed and edited the evening after my most recent fishing trip. What a challenge it turned out to be, for there were plenty of times, following a heavy mayfly hatch or an unforgettable summer downpour, when I found myself nodding off to sleep, ballpoint pen in hand, and long before my bed-time! There were many instances, as well, when my hand-written pages had only one or two hook-ups listed, but if I got "skunked," I dutifully added that humbling experience to all the rest. My motto for diary-keepers was "if it happened, save it." How are you going to get other anglers, let alone non-anglers, to take you seriously if you report only your most glorious triumphs?

Most writers who keep journals of their fishing trips are not doing so for their personal gratification. Instead, they're trying to become better anglers, and they will. Becoming a better writer is a different matter. Writing does not come easily to me or, for that matter, to most of the writers I have met. It does not seem to matter much whether a

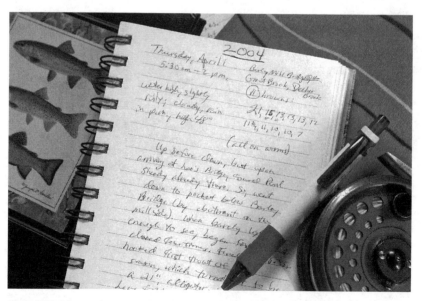

One of 30-some volumes of handwritten fishing logs maintained by the author beginning in the 1960s.

writer is hammering out a news article on deadline for a local morning paper, or putting some finishing touches on a somewhat scholarly book about climate change and its potential impact on recreational trout fisheries. A typical author, if there is such a creature, gets hung-up at his or her computer keyboard at some point. Suddenly, good ideas are hard to come by in the first place, and even more difficult to execute. College writing professors and newspaper editors, alike, have a few tricks for crashing through an old-fashioned "writer's block," but one of the most effective methods is to reach for an old, reliable information source, then re-read it, paragraph by paragraph, until the author with the problem finds a nugget of inspiration. Hemingway's "Big Two-Hearted River" always got me a real jumpstart when I needed one.

The serious diary-keeper may work harder than most other writers because much is expected of him. On occasion, he may even stay up late at night when his fishing buddies are tuckered out and snoring in their pillows. Before turning in, he will jot down the results of that day's action so that he can go to bed with a clear conscience. In the morning, somebody who arose in the dim, gray dawn and is pretending to be all bright-eyed and bushy-tailed will ask if he can peruse the diary. Depending on the inquirer's disposition and the narrative skills of the log-keeper, the book may be set aside after a few minutes or passed around half the morning. Months later, however, you or whoever else is the official historian at your fishing camp, will have no more notoriety than he or she who accepts the mantle of camp chef. (And, whether you knew it or not, the most admired person in your typical fishing camp is the chef, not the guide.)

Perhaps you aren't sure how to make good use of a fishing diary. If so, come along while I grab a couple of my thirty-some volumes and do a little "field work." Don't be surprised, however, if we occasionally pause to reminisce and rest. For one of the best properties associated with a long-running diary is its ability to stimulate memories—even those which the owner has virtually wiped clean from the slate. I am not exaggerating, in fact, when I tell you that my diary recollections include not only recent catches but also the smells and touches of primal things.

For example, when I start thumbing through the more recent volumes in my diary, the discovery of a decades-old report on a stream

I have not fished for many years turned into a flood of memories. Some of these recollections pertain to popular streams in western New York, and others are rooted in places less well-known. It hardly matters, if you think about it, because a trout stream is a place where trout live. Therefore, if you master the nuances of one creek by thoughtful observation, other streams will come into sharper focus. I can give you many examples of how this process works

As I wrote this chapter, I was thinking of a specific diary report— two of them, actually—which resulted from a pair of bittersweet fishing trips that took place in the early 80s. Taken in their entirety, these incidents are of great potential value to any angler who hears about them. Remember what I just said, a few paragraphs back, about one event leading to another. In this case, both incidents occurred in central New York, but the same sort of thing happens to other anglers in other sectors of the state, too.

Thinking back on these particular events, I remembered that they were spread over two consecutive opening days of the New York trout season. One of the highlights, for me at least, was the photo which my pal Dan Skinner took of the first day's catch. Unfortunately, I misplaced that picture at least 25 years ago, yet it is sharply etched in my consciousness. I could not forget it if I wished to do so, because Dan died of leukemia when he was just 35 years old. That sad day came round in 1983, according to a laminated obituary card that I have somehow managed to retain for all these years. A quick search through my diaries confirmed that the sequence of events that I remembered began in the spring of 1981.

In late March that year I happened to dial the number of a state fisheries manager to check on stream conditions and get an unbiased review of some small waters that might be worth a visit during the early part of the trout season. The DEC expert who happened to be on telephone duty that day knew area streams quite well, and passed along a few good tips. One bit of advice centered on Trout Brook in southern Cortland County. I had never fished it up to that point, and I doubted I would find time to take a swing at it two days hence. That happened to be April Fool's Day, which marked the beginning of that year's statewide trout season. I anticipated that most trout waters in the Syracuse area would be crowded with anglers that morning—and so they were.

OUR UNCLE IN ALBANY WANTS YOU

For decades, trout fishermen have been recruited to help the Department of Environmental Conservation's Bureau of Fisheries collect data which can be used to monitor population trends, good or bad, in New York's lakes and streams. It's all done by volunteers who either maintain an angler catch diary or simply submit to stream-side interviews conducted by summer technicians.

In recent years, valuable information has been supplied by boat, shoreline and tributary fishermen, most of whom keep detailed diary records of their outings in the Finger Lakes, Lake Ontario feeder streams, the upper Genesee River and Oatka Creek, among other trout fisheries. Not a few anglers have also volunteered to work side-by-side with DEC workers during electrofishing in rivers, creeks and brooks throughout the state.

Take it from me as a former regular keeper of facts for the DEC's Region 7 angler diary program, the state agency always can use some newbies. If you are interested, look up your regional field office and ask how you can help. The numbers you need can be found in "New York Freshwater Fishing," which is the same regulations book provided to anyone who purchases an Empire State fishing license.

It fell upon me, first, to give my home water, a popular Onondaga County stream, a serious couple of hours. But I arrived at the stream on that fateful morning to find that a single fisherman had somehow managed to beat me to "my" spot, which was just downstream from a picturesque waterfall. He told me later that he had seen me ring up a nice catch the previous year and gave himself a mental note to get up a little earlier next April. This time I watched him reel in three pretty browns, and a short while after that a friend of his showed up. The first early riser was a worm-dunker, and the fellow who joined him on the opposite side of the creek was a salted-minnow specialist who, a couple of minutes later, was into a strong fish of his own. Realizing both fellows were on their game that morning and having a lot of fun, I decided to reel in and try some place different.

Although my diary affirmed I had fished this pool below a falls on Nine Mile Creek on at least 10 consecutive opening days, I declined to feel sorry for myself and picked up my creel, which already had several decent browns in it. With no real regrets, I walked back up the slope, started my car and took off for Cortland County.

The creel limit in those times was 10 trout per day per angler, and I am embarrassed to say that in the early 1980s, I was one of many local fishermen who did not consider the season to be off to a good start until I had stacked a few trout in the freezer. But on this season-opener, the action was almost too fast, and as air temperatures climbed through the '60s and into the '70s, anglers began to show along every stream I passed. As I drove out into the countryside, I wondered how long it would take me to find that little brook trout stream my DEC friend had recommended.

As it turned out, the drive covered about 50 miles, but most of it was between two exit/entrance ramps on a federal highway. An hour away from home, I slid a garden worm on the barbed shank of a size 6 Eagle Claw hook and almost immediately felt a series of rat-tat tugs on my deep-drifting line. My first cast, and I was already into the brook trout.

I reeled in 13 brookies that day, and took home four, the largest of them an almost unimaginable native which measured 15 inches from stem to stern. To this day, that hook-jawed male is the largest wild brookie I have ever caught. None of those Opening Day fish, not the biggest nor even the smallest among them, had ever seen the inside of a fish hatchery. The colors were indescribably beautiful, and every fin was neatly tapered and sharp as a spear point. Too bad I had a new roll of black and white film in the camera Dan used to take my picture!

I'm sure most readers would agree that any stream that produces memories like these calls for a return trip, and the sooner the better. I invited my brother-in-law, Bill McPartland, to accompany me on the following opening day, but things did not work out as we had hoped.

After a couple of hours spent on Nine Mile Creek near Syracuse, we swore Bill to secrecy and headed for the brook trout dream stream.

At the end of the trip, we clambered out of Bill's sedan, put on our hip boots, creels and fishing vests, locked up the car, and took several steps from the road to the brook—and realized the keys were still in the ignition. By the time we retrieved them, and broke the driver's side window in the process, neither of us was in a mood to keep fishing. In those days, remember, practically nobody carried a phone in their car, although quite a few fishermen grudgingly admitted to having locked themselves out of their vehicles at one time or another. We might have called a nearby garage or even a state police substation for some advice, but this was a very rural location. For an hour or so, while we pondered how to get those car keys, I swore I heard a solo banjo player ("Brr-zhing-a-zhing-zhing-zhing") in the nearby woods, but that ominous noise was traced to a bluegrass band which was tuning up for a gig at a nearby country music theme park and campground.

Reading my 34-year-old accounting of these two trips, I realized the first outing was even better than I had remembered it. I can also see there is no point of annoying Bill by bringing up this sore subject within hearing distance of my sister, Karen. I must admit, she has treated him pretty well over the years, even on those occasions when he is hanging out with me.

That brook trout junket was not the only outing that I managed to ruin for Bill. Now that he's in a position to retire and do a little more trout fishing, I'm really hoping he will take a walk down Memory Lane, guided by fishing buddies and, at least to some degree, by his brother-in-law's angler diary.

CHAPTER TWELVE

The Aging Angler

My hands were shaking, and I was talking to myself. If that wasn't bad enough, anyone who had been within hearing range a few minutes earlier would have been shocked at the variety of cuss words that rolled over my tongue. It was a pointless rant, directed at my inability to cope with the gradual erosion of skills that is part and parcel of every fly-fisher's life. To sum it up, a nasty spring storm was brewing, and the sky to the west of my fishing spot on Oatka Creek was ominously dark. My first inclination was to select a dry fly that was a reasonable match for the Hendrickson mayflies that had started to emerge from the creek 10 or 15 minutes earlier, get in a few casts before the clouds burst, then sprint for the car. It would have been a workable plan, except for the fact that I could not see my fly nor the 5X tippet that should have slipped easily through the eye of the hook. I had forgotten to bring the head lamp and the flip-down magnifying glass which, placed on the baseball cap I usually wore on-stream, made knot-tying chores manageable.

The thunder that drew ever closer did nothing for my confidence, which was scant to begin with. Knowing that I had become a bit care-less at my fly-tying bench in recent years, I looked in vain for a floating pattern with a hook-eye that was not overwrapped with thread or plugged with head cement. I tried to make a secure connection with half a dozen versions of the fabled Hendrickson, and finally gave up. Thunder is merely noise, but I don't take chances with lightning. My fishing partner and I turned in the direction of the car when the crack-ling light show started. I reeled up line and leader as I stumbled up the path, and breathed a deep sigh of relief when I opened the car door and felt the rain, just starting to spatter on the windshield.

As a young fisherman, I sometimes made decisions that were daring, if not quite reckless. In those days, during my 20s and early 30s, I did not ignore the dangers associated with my fly-fishing passion, but often weighed one risk against another. After all, what were the odds that I might actually be struck by lightning? It had never happened to me or my fishing pals, not even once, so why should this evening produce different results?

If I had tied on a fresh fly in advance of that storm, instead of being surprised by the sudden arrival of thunder, lightning and powerful gusts of wind, I might have given in to this daredevil mood. Luckily, it all happened so fast that I was virtually forced to retreat, and instead of getting soaked to the skin, my friend and I sat in the pickup truck while the heavens hammered the roof with rain, hail and, finally gave us a few minutes of calm between storms. It kept raining long after sunset, but we were safe, dry and humbly aware that none of us is as young as we used to be.

What really put me in a funk, however, was the steady stream of gadgets and gizmos which kept finding their way out of my tackle vest. Most of these were hard to find tools listed in fly-fishing catalogs or at online shopping addresses, and thus were not easy to order, receive and replace. Consequently, I had come to rely on fishing partners who kept two or three of everything, knowing I was bound to need these items before they did. The fact they had enough seconds and thirds of this or that made me feel like a bit of a leech, but at least I had somebody I could tap for tackle in an emergency—maybe. It was almost like going shopping, myself, which was something I seldom did unless I had to.

More upsetting, by far, was the gradual, embarrassing erosion of my fishing skills.

At first I was in denial, but it gradually became obvious to anybody who had known me for very long that I took longer to tie knots than I used to, if I could finish them at all. It was simply infuriating to spend five or even 10 minutes to complete a clinch knot, let along an improved clinch, which had been my standard hook-to-tippet connection for many trout seasons.

Most annoying to me was my inability to change dry flies in the fading light of the evening, when trout are most apt to feed on the surface. The hardest task was poking the end of the monofilament through a hook eye. Somewhere I must have lost the depth perception necessary to do that particular job. A year earlier, as I recalled, knots did not cause so much of a problem. Now, however, they were nearly impossible at times, and whenever I was leaving for a big trip I prayed that the nicer fish at my destination would pick their menu and get to feasting while I was taking my time with the knots.

Just as the storm struck Oatka Creek and the gigantic local willow trees began to whipsaw back and forth in the moaning wind, I had a very childish tantrum and hurled my remaining supply of comparadun-style Hendrickson dry flies at the ground and stumbled in the direction of the closest fisherman parking area. That's how discouraged and disgusted I was with my recent, personal performance while on a trout stream.

I felt so tired and nervous, that evening, that I had a disturbing nightmare about swapping my fly rods for a new set of golf clubs. A good thing I didn't follow-through on that one, huh?

If there were any lingering doubts as to the nature and cause of my trout-angling woes, they were dispelled by another dream a few nights later. After awaking with a start, I visited the refrigerator and then scanned my medicine cabinet for something that would be helpful yet harmless to a sleep-deprived, aging trout fisherman. Nothing I had quite fit the bill, so I shut the cabinet and glanced in the mirror on the outside of the door. Staring back at me was somebody I hadn't paid much notice, lately. It was me, but not the old me. The face was my own, of course, but I scarcely recognized the wrinkles, the unruly shock of gray hair, or the faint liver spots on my left temple.

I blinked and stared once more at the looking glass, ruefully. When did I get this way, I wondered? Well, I had to admit it didn't happen overnight. I had acquired my receding hairline one strand at a time; and my puffy eyes were the logical result of delicious dinners and many more second helpings and desserts than anybody should consume. Many of those meals were washed down with premium beers or perfectly chilled bottles of wine. I chuckled at such memories. They were happy times, and whether my wife and I had dined on the town or at home on a cold winter's night didn't matter.

At that remembrance I smiled back at myself. I really could eat, and I needed to cut back on my dinners and snacks, alike. It was also time I began to recalibrate and fine-tune my fishing and fly-tying techniques, but it was far too soon to hang up my rod. In the year that followed, I trained myself to make my fishing time easier and more enjoyable, by recognizing what could be changed and accepting what could not. Gradually, I came to know that "real me" in the mirror, and liked what I saw. Okay, maybe "liked" is a bit much. A more appropriate word would be "tolerated."

We are all aging anglers, although some of us are clearly faster than others. Like athletes, we reach our personal peak performance levels in our 30s or thereabouts. Then we resist or patiently endure the inevitable long, slow decline in fishing skills and knowledge. Out of fear or actual need, we enter middle age and then old age with caution in regard to our passionate pursuits. By the time we hit 50, most of us are inclined, already, to avoid the swift and slippery stretches of water on our favorite rivers and streams, even those which we recently waded with aplomb.

Some wait until their 50th or even 60th birthdays for the logical next step but I have used a wading staff of some sort since I finished high school, and if you ever come along on one of my trout trips, I will have a spare staff for your use—if you desire to try it, of course. The wading staff has kept me from taking many tumbles over the years, some in the water and not a few on dry land. I have used it to poke carefully into the tall grass in snake country, and have also leaned hard against the stick when I suddenly felt my balance slip-sliding away on an algae-cloaked boulder or an eroding trail.

The unshakeable staffs became my regular river companions long ago, mainly because I frequented pocket water at every opportunity back when I had a much thicker head of hair and a trimmer waist-line. I quickly recognized that this simple tool had the potential to save my life one day, and not necessarily during the twilight of my trout fishing career, either. As I entered my second decade of dealing with

Parkinson's disease, my good old "stick on a rope" seemed more vital than ever. Good doctors and prayerful parishioners deserve much of the credit for my ability to deal with this demon, but I also admire the many folks who have stood by my determination to stand up!

Somewhere, deep down, I know Parkinson's or perhaps the aging process in general will force me to curb swift-water fishing or even give it up completely. But that day needn't be tomorrow. It could be 10 more years, or five more tacked onto that. I will do my best, for as long as I can, that I may keep up my friendships with the rivers and rivulets I have always loved.

AS LONG AS YOUR TIRED OLD EYES WILL LET YOU

The older I get, the more I appreciate the critical importance of good vision to squinty-eyed trout fishers like you and me. When I was 40 and even 50 years old, I had no problem at all knotting a minuscule trout fly to the end of a tapered leader. I lost that degree of hand-to-eye coordination gradually, but by the time I was 60, I was terrified I might have fallen so far behind that I might never catch up.

At one point, I became so desperate that I seriously considered hiring a much younger angler to come along to the streams in my area of New York and do my knot-tying! In other words, I thought I needed an Scottish-style ghillie. But how else could I possibly keep going after surface-feeding trout—my favorite participant sport— the way I always had, by mentally sorting through the bugs that drifted on the river's currents and then calmly browsing through the contents of my fly vest—for imitations of the right size, shape, color and movement?

Fortunately, where there's a will, there's a way, and after lots of small failures and a few promising experiments, I finally put together a system for adding and subtracting terminal tackle to the business end of my trout-fishing rig. Although I still have to struggle a bit at twilight or during heavy rain showers, I at least can get the job done with confidence, instead of going into a cold-sweat panic just as the big hatch is getting into high gear.

The tools we wise old anglers need for making knots, tippets, and such work for us on the water instead of looking for a picnic table or some other stable platform, include a shore-fisherman's head lamp, a hard-plastic magnifier to clip to the brim of your base-ball or painter's cap, and a set of miniature bobbins that you can rely on to poke your fly-fishing leader tippet through a hook eye.

You've got a couple of personal choices if you want to dig a little deeper into the knot thing. There are all sorts of tools avail-able through catalogs and the "big box" stores across the country, such as Bass Pro Shops, Gander Mountain and Dick's. All of their knot tools work according to directions, but you may not need them if you supplement your bag of tricks with a bottle of Sally Hansen Hard as Nails. Yet, there is more than one way to link fly hooks and leaders with nail polish. For example, you could purchase a small bottle of black or white quick-drying nail polish—the color depends on your visual background—and dab it on the last 2 inches of your tippet. Let it dry for 30 seconds or so, then tie your intended knot. Snip your left-over tippet just beyond where the polish dried.

Sometimes, we fly fishers get so rattled by this tying one on that we hurry through it, and cause our hook and tippet to split from each other, necessitating a do-over. Way back in the early 1990s, when I wrote an article about the fly-fishing school Lee and Joan Wulff operated in the Catskills, Joan demonstrated an easy way to tie a better clinch knot. She merely poked her tippet through the eye, perhaps 3 inches—just enough for her to tie a nifty over-hand knot. If that knot should start to slip, it merely pulled tight so that the tiny ball sat snugly against the tippet.

Worked like a charm. No wonder Joan is known, to this day, as "The First Lady of Fly-fishing!"

Fishing Regulations for Western New York Trout Streams

The six counties that comprise western New York—also known as Department of Environmental Conservation Region 9—have very few special regulations to confuse trout fishers. Anglers who schedule trips to the trout waters in those counties—Chautauqua, Allegany, Cattaraugus, Wyoming, Erie and Niagara—can quickly find what rules they need to know by consulting the state's Freshwater Fishing booklet that is made available at no extra cost to anyone who purchases a New York fishing license.

The statewide regulations for trout-fishing include a season that opens on April 1 and ends October 15, and a creel limit of five trout per day, of which only two can be more than 12 inches long.

The following special regulations apply to certain trout streams in Region 6 counties as of March 31, 2016.

Allegany County: In the *Genesee River* from the Route 19 bridge at Shongo downstream for a distance of 2.5 miles, trout fishing is permitted all year on a catch and release basis. Only artificial lures or flies may be used.

From the no-kill at Shongo and upstream to the Pennsylvania state line; and downstream from the no-kill to the dam at Belmont, standard New York regulations are in force. That is, the daily limit is five trout of any size, but only two of the five may exceed 12 inches in length. Bait, lures and flies may be used.

In the Allegany County section of *Wiscoy Creek*, anglers may creel three trout of 10 inches or more, daily, from April 1–October 15. During the off-season, from October 16 through March 31, catch-and-release fishing for trout is permitted on the creek, using artificial flies or lures only.

Angling for trout is permitted on *East Koy* and *Chenunda* creeks from April 1 through October 15. The limit on both streams during this period is five trout a day, of which two may exceed 12 inches. During the off season, Oct. 16–March 31, only artificial lures or flies may be used and fishing is catch-and-release, only.

Cattaraugus County: In Allegany State Park, park rules may change from year to year for individual streams and anglers should always double-check at the park office near Salamanca. In most years, streams within the park are open to trout fishers year-round, but the creel limit from April 1 through October 15 is five of any size, of which no more than two can be longer than 12 inches. Also, from October 16 through March 31, park streams are no-kill only and fishermen must use either artificial flies or lures. Some stocked streams in the park are governed by "Delayed Harvest" rules, which stipulate that anglers must release all trout caught in said waters prior to a set date. After that, trout caught in those streams may be creeled. *Anglers should check with the park office to find out which waters are subject to Delayed Harvest regulations.*

In *Clear Creek* upstream from the Wyoming-Cattaraugus county line, as well as *Lime Lake Outlet* and *McKinstry Creek,* during the April 1–October 15 regular season, anglers may creel up to five trout a day, but all must be at least nine inches long and no more than two can be longer than 12 inches. From October 16 through March 31, you can fish this trio of streams, catch-and-release, with artificial lures or flies, only.

Also, *in Elm Creek, Elton Creek, Mansfield Creek, Clear Creek (Ellington), Fenton Brook and Cattaraugus Creek* upstream of the Springville dam, the creel limit is 5 a day of any size, except no more than 2 a day can be longer than 12 inches.

In all *Allegany State Park* waters except for Red House Lake and Quaker Lake, the regulations allow anglers to keep up to five trout a day of any size, except that only two of an individual's "keepers" may be longer than 12 inches.

Chautauqua County: In *Goose Creek*, trout fishing is allowed all year and anglers may keep five trout per day of any size; however, no more than two of the five may be longer than 12 inches.

In *Clear Creek (Ellington)* and *Prendergast Creek*, from April 1– October 15, anglers may keep five trout a day but no more than two of those can be longer than 12 inches. Between the state-standard trout seasons, from Oct. 16 through March 15, trout fishing is allowed on a catch-and-release basis, and fishing tackle is limited to artificial flies or lures.

Erie County: In *Lake Erie*, the *Niagara River,* and their tributaries upstream to impassable barriers, as well as *Cattaraugus Creek* below the Springville dam, and also in the Buffalo River and tributaries, downstream of the first impassable barrier—all angling is governed by Great Lakes regulations.

In *Hosmer (Sardinia) Brook*, fishing for trout is allowed all year. From April 1 through October 15, the limit is five trout per day of at least 9 inches, but only two of the five may be longer than 12 inches. The rules from April through mid-October are catch-and-release with only artificial flies or lures permitted.

Trout fishing is allowed all year *in Cattaraugus Creek* upstream from the Springville dam. From April 1 through Oct. 15, the creel limit is five a day of any size, provided the limit includes no more than two trout longer than 12 inches. From October 16 through March 31, fishing in the "Cat" upstream from the dam is catch-and-release, and anglers are restricted to the use of artificial flies and lures only.

Wyoming County: In that part of *Wiscoy Creek* which is between a marker half a mile upstream of the East Hillside Road bridge and another marker half a mile downstream of the same structure, fishing is year-round, catch-and-release and artificial lures or flies, only.

The remainder of the creek within Wyoming County is subject to a three-per-day trout limit from April 1 through Oct. 15. Creeled fish must be at least 10 inches long and no more than two of the creeled trout may exceed 12 inches. In the same section, catch-and-release fishing, lures or flies only is permitted from October 16 through March 31.

In *Clear Creek*, from its mouth to the Wyoming-Cattaraugus county line, trout fishing is allowed from April 1 through Oct. 15 with a daily catch limit of five trout. The minimum length is 9 inches but no more than two of the five can exceed 12 inches in length. Between Oct. 16 through March 31, the same stretch of the creek is regulated as catch-and-release, artificial flies or lures only.

East Koy Creek, Cattaraugus Creek upstream from the dam at Springville and the Wyoming County section of *Oatka Creek* all have the same trout seasons. From April 1 through October 15, the limit on each stream is five trout a day of any size but the creeled catch can't include more than two trout over 12 inches. From Oct. 16 through March 31, only catch-and-release fishing is allowed and participating anglers are limited to fishing with artificial lures or flies.

INDEX